THE WAY
PEOPLE
LIVE

Life
During the
Russian
Revolution

Titles in The Way People Live series include:

THE WAY
PEOPLE
LIVE

Life During the Russian Revolution

by Victoria Sherrow

Lucent Books, P.O. Box 289011, San Diego, CA 92198-9011

Library of Congress Cataloging-in-Publication Data

Sherrow, Victoria.
    Life during the Russian Revolution / by Victoria Sherrow.
        p.   cm. — (The way people live)
    Includes bibliographical references and index.
    Summary: Discusses the background, historical context, events, and way
of life of the Russian Revolution.
    ISBN 1-56006-389-0 (lib. : alk. paper)
    1. Soviet Union—History—Revolution, 1917–1921—Juvenile literature.
[1. Soviet Union—History—Revolution, 1917–1921.]   I. Title.   II. Series.
DK265.S444   1998
947.084'1—dc21   97–51181
                                                                                CIP
                                                                                 AC

Contents

Discovering the Humanity in Us All

The Way People Live series focuses on pockets of human culture. Some of these are current cultures, like the Eskimos of the Arctic; others no longer exist, such as the Jewish ghetto in Warsaw during World War II. What many of these cultural pockets share, however, is the fact that they have been viewed before, but not completely understood.

To really understand any culture, it is necessary to strip the mind of the common notions we hold about groups of people. These stereotypes are the archenemies of learning. It does not even matter whether the stereotypes are positive or negative; they are confining and tight. Removing them is a challenge that's not easily met, as anyone who has ever tried it will admit. Ideas that do not fit into the templates we create are unwelcome visitors—ones we would prefer remain quietly in a corner or forgotten room.

The cowboy of the Old West is a good example of such confining roles. The cowboy was courageous, yet soft-spoken. His time (it is always a he, in our template) was spent alternatively saving a rancher's daughter from certain death on a runaway stagecoach, or shooting it out with rustlers. At times, of course, he was likely to get a little crazy in town after a trail drive, but for the most part, he was the epitome of inner strength. It is disconcerting to find out that the cowboy is human, even a bit childish. Can it really be true that cowboys would line up to help the cook on the trail drive grind coffee, just hoping he would give them a little stick of pep-

permint candy that came with the coffee shipment? The idea of tough cowboys vying with one another to help "Coosie" (as they called their cooks) for a bit of candy seems silly and out of place.

So is the vision of Eskimos playing video games and watching MTV, living in prefab housing in the Arctic. It just does not fit with what "Eskimo" means. We are far more comfortable with snow igloos and whale blubber, harpoons and kayaks.

Although the cultures dealt with in Lucent's The Way People Live series are often historically and socially well known, the emphasis is on the personal aspects of life. Groups of people, while unquestionably affected by their politics and their governmental structures, are more than those institutions. How do people in a particular time and place educate their children? What do they eat? And how do they build their houses? What kinds of work do they do? What kinds of games do they enjoy? The answers to these questions bring these cultures to life. People's lives are revealed in the particulars and only by knowing the particulars can we understand these cultures' will to survive and their moments of weakness and greatness.

This is not to say that understanding politics does not help to understand a culture. There is no question that the Warsaw ghetto, for example, was a culture that was brought about by the politics and social ideas of Adolf Hitler and the Third Reich. But the Jews who were crowded together in the ghetto cannot be understood by the Reich's politics. Their life was a day-to-day battle for existence, and the creativity and methods they used to prolong their lives is a vital story of human perseverance that would be denied by focusing only on the institutions of Hitler's Germany. Knowing that children as young as five or six outwitted Nazi guards on a daily basis, that Jewish policemen helped the Germans control the ghetto, that children attended secret schools in the ghetto and even earned diplomas—these are the things that reveal the fabric of life, that can inspire, intrigue, and amaze.

Books in The Way People Live series allow both the casual reader and the student to see humans as victims, heroes, and onlookers. And although humans act in ways that can fill us with feelings of sorrow and revulsion, it is important to remember that "hero," "predator," and "victim" are dangerous terms. Heaping undue pity or praise on people reduces them to objects, and strips them of their humanity.

Seeing the Jews of Warsaw only as victims is to deny their humanity. Seeing them only as they appear in surviving photos, staring at the camera with infinite sadness, is limiting, both to them and to those who want to understand them. To an object of pity, the only appropriate response becomes "Those poor creatures!" and that reduces both the quality of their struggle and the depth of their despair. No one is served by such two-dimensional views of people and their cultures.

With this in mind, The Way People Live series strives to flesh out the traditional, two-dimensional views of people in various cultures and historical circumstances. Using a wide variety of primary quotations—the words not only of the politicians and government leaders, but of the real people whose lives are being examined—each book in the series attempts to show an honest and complete picture of a culture removed from our own by time or space.

By examining cultures in this way, the reader will notice not only the glaring differences from his or her own culture, but also will be struck by the similarities. For indeed, people share common needs—warmth, good company, stability, and affirmation from others. Ultimately, seeing how people really live, or have lived can only enrich our understanding of ourselves.

A Sharp Turn in History

People in Russia are used to cold weather, but the winter of 1916–1917 was unusually severe. Temperatures plunged as low as forty degrees below zero. Fuel, needed more than ever, was scarce. During the numerous labor strikes, workers did not show up at railroad stations or shipyards. City streetcars did not run. Factories stood idle, so fewer goods were produced.

Factory goods, along with food and fuel, often did not reach their destinations because of transportation problems, which were aggravated by the weather. At one point, the pipes of twelve hundred locomotives froze and burst. These trains were removed from service for weeks while they underwent repairs. Fewer trains meant that even less fuel, food, and manufactured goods reached the people.

The bitter weather matched the mood of many Russians that February. People in the countryside lacked matches, cloth goods, boots, metal pots, and tools they used to run their farms. City dwellers lacked grain and other farm produce. Workers labored long hours for low wages, then returned in the darkness to their cold apartments, wondering what they would eat the next day.

Hunger became rampant as food prices increased by about 50 percent during those months. Russians who could afford food stood in long lines in the snow to buy bread or a few turnips or potatoes. Often, they waited for nothing. There were no signs that things would improve. Russian money steadily lost its value as prices rose.

Frustration exploded into anger, aimed at rulers who seemed unable to understand or resolve these problems. Many people were also furious that their leaders had involved Russia in a world war since 1914. The war had further drained the country of food, clothing, fuel, and other resources. Millions of people had lost husbands, sons, fathers, and brothers at the war front.

In Petrograd (called St. Petersburg before the war), tensions rose as lines lengthened outside bakeries and markets. Thousands of people marched in the streets holding signs that read "Give us bread!" "Down with the Autocracy!" "We Want Peace!" More and more striking workers joined students and other protesters.

An Absolute Monarchy

This was not the first time the Russian people had expressed dissatisfaction toward their leaders. Unlike neighboring countries in Europe, which had developed more representative forms of government, Russia entered the twentieth century with an absolutist monarchy. In charge of this vast land was one person: the czar.

Czarism dated back to 1547, hundreds of years before the Russian Revolution. Ivan the Terrible had expanded his kingdom—Moscow and its vicinity—to include all of Russia. He set up an autocratic government headed by a czar, which is the Russian word for Caesar. The czar,

Angry crowds were a familiar sight in Russian cities during World War I. Most of these mobs were upset with the monarchy, which appeared to care very little for the problems of the commoners.

or emperor, claimed to have absolute power ordained by God. Russian law declared that the ruler was "beyond reproach." In 1716, under Czar Peter I, known as Peter the Great, the law was written as follows:

> His Majesty is an absolute monarch, who is not obliged to answer for his actions to anyone in the world but has the power and the authority to govern his states and lands as a Christian sovereign, in accord with his desire and goodwill.[1]

The czar acted as both ruler and proprietor of the country, and many Russians accepted this system, or felt powerless to change it. Czarism also reflected the paternalistic (male-dominated) arrangement that existed in Russian households and villages.

In imperial Russia, people lived under a huge, complicated bureaucracy. The czar and his designates controlled the government, economy, military, and religious institutions. The government owned most of the factories and farms and was the nation's largest employer, controlling trade and money. Only people who served as officers or administrators could attain a noble rank.

Both the middle class and working class were smaller than those in other westernized countries. Though nobles made up less than 1 percent of the population, they controlled

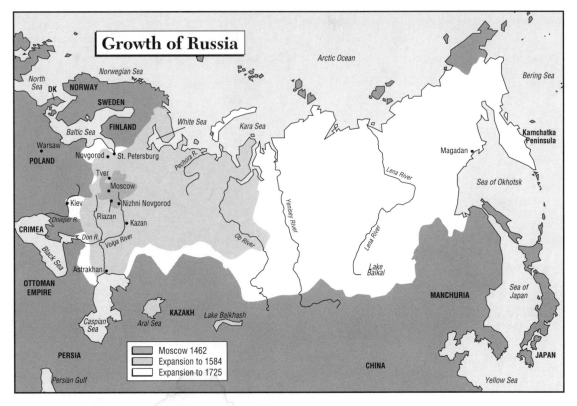

Growth of Russia

Moscow 1462
Expansion to 1584
Expansion to 1725

most of Russia's wealth. The labor of the poor supported wealthy landowners and filled the imperial treasury.

The Long Road to Revolution

For more than one hundred years, people in Russia had protested against the regime, despite strict laws that banned political dissent. From time to time, groups and individuals planned to overthrow the czar; some used bullets and bombs to assassinate various leaders. None of these efforts gained enough support to spark a revolution.

The immense size and diversity of Russia help to explain why a revolution did not occur sooner. One hundred fifty million Russians inhabited land that stretched four thousand miles from Europe in the west to the Pacific

Ocean in the east, much of it flat plains or forestland. Along the eastern frontier, the Ural Mountains separated European Russia from Siberia. The people living in the Russian Empire were also quite diverse—Slavs, Balts, Turks, Germans, Armenians, Tartars, Uzbeks, and Georgians, among others.

Peasants, who made up about 80 percent of the population, lived in rural villages and were isolated from other people in many ways. Although many peasants disliked rich landowners and government officials, most were loyal to their czar and to the Russian Orthodox Church. They had little or no education and lacked political and economic power. Before the 1900s, people in rural areas seldom heard about the political ideas that had shaped other countries into democracies or constitutional monarchies; the vast majority were illiterate and could not read revolutionary

Workers of the World Unite

During the late 1800s, Russian intellectuals were drawn to new ideas about politics, economics, and social justice. The ideas of Karl Marx, who addressed the problems of industrialization, appealed to some of them during these changing times.

Karl Marx was born in Germany in 1818. After studying at various German universities, he became a writer and newspaper editor. He lost his job in 1843 after he began writing articles that strongly criticized the government.

Marx moved to Paris and continued to study philosophy, history, and political science. He was drawn to communism, a political system based on materialism—a belief that disregards spirituality in favor of the physical world. Marx stressed the importance of the labor that goes into producing food, housing, tools, and other necessities. In his view, capitalist factory owners exploited workers, just as feudal landowners had exploited serfs in medieval times. In a just system, said Marx, people benefit from what they produce in proportion to what they contribute to the final product. In 1844, Marx collaborated with Friedrich Engels, who shared his opinions. Together, they set forth principles of communism and called for a worldwide working-class movement that would achieve this new political and economic order. They believed workers would unite to drive out capitalists, leading to a classless society. Freedom and justice would follow as people worked for the good of the whole community and received in return the things they needed.

Ordered to leave Paris, Marx moved to Brussels, where he organized revolutionary groups that merged into the Communist League in 1847. The following year Marx and Engels wrote *The Communist Manifesto*, which became the authoritative statement on modern socialist philosophy. A political exile for most of his life, Marx continued to publish new papers and books and organize conferences. He died in 1883, before his theories gained their greatest influence.

The industrial revolution came late to Russia, and as the country went through those changes during the 1890s, Marxism made sense to some people. Russians who viewed themselves as worldly also liked the idea that Marxism was European and modern. Communist theories offered a comprehensive framework for how society operates and gave a clear plan for the future.

Marx said that this new system would require action to become reality. In 1845, he wrote, "The philosophers have only interpreted the world in various ways; the point, however, is to change it."

By 1905 at least three Marxist organizations existed in Russia. One group, called legalists, supported a moderate program of political and economic reforms. A second group, the Mensheviks, thought a revolution was necessary. The most radical group, the Bolsheviks, openly supported revolution. The name of the chief Bolshevik leader would become synonymous with the Russian Revolution: Lenin.

Karl Marx was a social critic who, along with Friedrich Engels, set down the principles of the communist movement that influenced the Russian Revolution.

literature. Peasants also worked hard to survive and thus had little time for revolutionary activities.

Nonetheless, Russian peasants occasionally rebelled against high taxes and cruel or unjust treatment. The government always managed to subdue them, often with brutal force. These waves of anger were unplanned and scattered. Masses of peasants did not unite or join other groups to overthrow the government.

However, by 1917, several changes had occurred. The industrial revolution had reached Russia, and many peasants had moved to work in the cities. About one-third of Russia's workers had ties to rural areas, and some 6 million left the cities at harvest time to work on farms. The working class steadily grew, and became more educated, class conscious, and politically informed. Most were young, energetic, and open to new ideas.

Russian soldiers who had served in more liberal nations, such as France, also questioned czarism. World War I (1914–1918) and the poor economy upset millions of people, including soldiers in the Russian army. Czar Nicholas II and his advisers made other decisions that angered people at all levels of society, and the czar and his German-born wife became increasingly unpopular. More middle-class Russians spoke out against a system in which a few people held wealth and power while poverty afflicted so many. In such an atmosphere, revolutionary ideas gained support.

From Czarism to Communism

Within just three days, the February revolution of 1917 would topple a mighty, three-hundred-year-old monarchy. This amazing turnover that started as a rebellion in one city grew into a mass movement. In the following months, political groups vied for the power once held by the czars. The Bolsheviks (later called Communists) sought not just to implement specific economic and political reforms, but to revolutionize the whole structure of the nation. The Bolshevik revolution that began that autumn continued for several years.

After a bloody civil war, a powerful new government assumed sweeping power over the Russian people. Bolshevik leaders had promised peace, bread, social equality, land for peasants, and better wages and working conditions. However, the new order also brought dissension, famine, and repressive laws backed by broad police power. When the revolution ended, the Russian people once again lived in a totalitarian system, only this time with different leaders. These events would have profound effects on Russia and the rest of the world for decades to come.

Leon Trotsky, a Bolshevik leader in the revolution, would later say, "You will not find another such sharp turn in history, especially if you remember that it involves a nation of 150 million people."[2]

The Czar Is Far Away: Rural Life in Czarist Russia

On the eve of the revolution, millions of the poorest Russians were living in the countryside. These people lived in Greater Russia as well as other parts of the Russian Empire, including Poland, Ukraine, and the Baltics. Most rural Russians, including peasants and Cossacks, worked as farmers, while rural Jews, banned from farming, worked in other trades and occupations.

Most peasants followed a way of life based on subsistence farming. Peasants, who made up about 80 percent of the population, had experienced centuries of autocratic rule and repression. A system of serfdom had evolved in Russia, as it had throughout Europe during the Middle Ages. The effects of serfdom lingered at the turn of the century.

Serfs and Peasants

The last census taken in Russia before serfdom was abolished in 1861 showed that, in a population of 60 million, there were 12 million free people. They included *dvoriane* (nobles and members of the upper class), the clergy, burghers (city dwellers), Cossacks, and independent farmers. The other 48 million were divided almost equally between state peasants and serfs.

State peasants were bound to the land but were not "property" in the same sense as serfs. They lived on estates owned by the monarchy or by people their rulers had named as government officials. Although state peasants were forbidden to leave their

Roughly four-fifths of Russia's population was composed of peasants and serfs. Peasant farmers (pictured here) fared better than their serf counterparts because they had freedom to change occupations and even set up and participate in local government.

villages without permission, they were otherwise free.

Laws passed in the 1830s permitted state peasants to hold title to their land and to practice limited, local self-government. Peasants who did not want to farm left their communes—village-owned land—although they were still required to pay taxes and a share of the rent. By paying a fee, a peasant could obtain a license to become a tradesman. Many became peddlers or found jobs in city factories or in mining, for example. Eventually, some state peasants became merchants, miners, factory workers, and even factory owners.

Some peasants leased their land to others and started small businesses. Tradespeople, such as masons and carpenters, sometimes formed cooperative work groups, doing jobs under contract for private customers and dividing the profits among members of the group.

Yet these individuals were still legally classified as peasants in imperial Russia. People who were born peasants remained so regardless of their occupation or where they

Free Warriors: The Cossacks

Among the free people living in rural Russia were the Cossacks, who settled in the southern plains of Russia. Their name comes from the word *kazak*, which means "free warrior." Czars permitted the Cossacks to live on their rich lands in exchange for serving in the imperial army. The men distinguished themselves as horsemen and warriors and were specially assigned to serve as guards for the imperial family and royal estates. Cossack soldiers were often mobilized to quiet unrest in cities and rural areas.

Nikita Yovich was one of sixteen children born to a family in the land of the Kuban Cossacks. His ancestors were Russians who refused to be serfs and fled to a region in the south where bands of Turks roamed. In Richard Lourie's *Russia Speaks: An Oral History from the Revolution*, Yovich describes the Cossack way of life:

My father was an ordinary Cossack, a noncommissioned officer. Every Cossack had to serve four years active duty in the army and you were in the reserves until you were thirty-three. A Cossack was responsible for his own horse and equipment, everything except for weapons. Once a year there'd be a general meeting and a Cossack would have to show what shape his equipment was in. . . .

Every Cossack worked the land. There were no factories where we lived. Just grain mills, sugar plants, [and] creameries. Cossacks were farmers. The Cossacks were different from the rest of Russia and all the rest of the world—Cossacks didn't own their land. The land belonged to the Cossack community and when a male Cossack reached seventeen, he was apportioned his share. Women were not given land.

In the tight-knit Cossack communities, pressure was placed on men who did not fulfill their duties as husbands and fathers. A leader called the *ataman* would strip such a man of his rank of Cossack, and he could be sent to Siberia. Religious observances were also a regular part of Cossack life. Most Cossacks were literate and finished secondary school.

lived. Russian law, dating back to medieval times, defined social status in terms of what was called the "Estate," which people were born into or which they reached by achieving a certain military or civil service rank. This status was listed in people's passports, which were required when traveling inside the country as well as abroad.

Besides peasant, these classifications included merchant, burgher, noble, and cleric. Until the early 1900s, peasants could not change this status unless their commune released them from their obligations as taxpaying members.

A Meager Existence with No Civil Rights

Serfs lived mostly in the central and western provinces. They were not slaves in the usual sense. Though serfs were attached to the land, the land was considered as property, not the people themselves. In addition, their work was supervised by older family members, not by slave masters or overseers. It was illegal to trade or sell serfs, although some landlords broke this law. Most local authorities ignored laws that banned serfs from owning property, and many owned their homes. Serfs' land was often located beside the estate-owned land; the crops they raised on this land were for their own use.

Some observers concluded that Russian peasants were better off than poor peasants or laborers in other countries. Russian Aleksandr Pushkin wrote,

In Russia there is not one man who does not have his *own* living quarters. A poor man who goes into the world leaves *his* izba [hut]. This does not exist in other countries. Everywhere in Europe to own

a cow is a sign of luxury; in Russia not to have one is a sign of dreadful poverty.[3]

Foreign visitors made similar remarks. In 1820, an English sea captain named John Dundas Cochrane wrote,

The condition of the peasantry here is far superior to that class in Ireland. In Russia, provisions are plentiful, good and cheap; while in Ireland they are scanty, poor, and [expensive], the best part being exported. . . . Good comfortable log-houses are here found in every village, immense droves of cattle are scattered over an unlimited pasture, and whole forests of fuel may be obtained for a trifle.[4]

British writer Robert Bremner visited Russia planning to expose the plight of the peasants. However, in 1839 he wrote,

His food may be coarse; but he has an abundance of it. His hut may be homely; but it is dry and warm. We are apt to fancy that if our peasantry be badly off, we can at least flatter ourselves with the assurance that they are much more comfortable than those of foreign countries. But this is a gross delusion.[5]

However, as observers also noted, peasants in other countries had civil rights, including the right to buy and sell property, travel freely, follow a profession of their choice, and pursue education. Russian peasants had no such rights. Although most landlords behaved decently, some were cruel and oppressive. Marriage rights were a big area of contention. Landlords preferred that a serf marry young, to a mate of the landlord's choice, so they could obtain additional labor. Bitter conflicts also erupted over the ownership

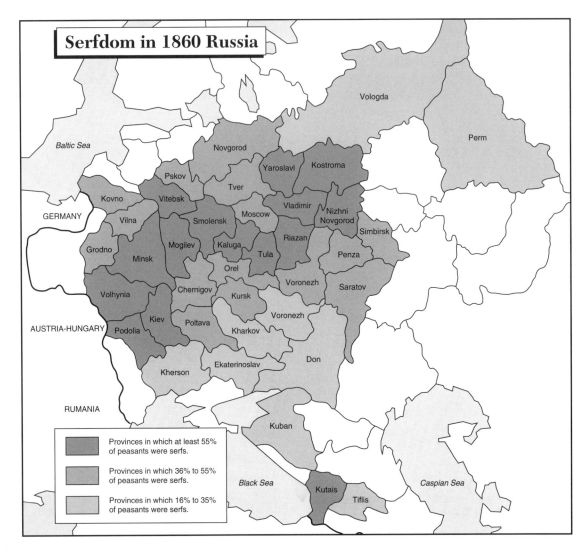

Serfdom in 1860 Russia

Provinces in which at least 55% of peasants were serfs.

Provinces in which 36% to 55% of peasants were serfs.

Provinces in which 16% to 35% of peasants were serfs.

of land. Peasants believed the land should belong to those who tilled the soil, not to those who merely had the money to buy it.

Continuing Poverty

Even after Czar Alexander II freed the serfs in 1861, old customs and restrictions remained. Peasants coped with their situation in different ways. Many complained about landlords and bureaucrats but took no decisive ac-

tion. When famine hit the countryside, young men went to the cities seeking work. Some, especially younger peasants, wanted to own land instead of sharing it with their neighbors in the communal system that the government had devised. Thousands of peasants broke the law against leaving their villages and moved to sparsely populated Siberia to start farms.

Although they were "liberated," most peasants remained wretchedly poor. Farming was a way to eke out a living but did not yield extra income. During years when rainfall was scant or when insects attacked crops, peasants went hungry. They often lacked enough land to feed themselves and their families, especially as the population grew and farming methods and tools remained crude.

During the short (four to six months) growing season, peasants raised mostly grain—rye, oats, and wheat. On northern farms, oats was the main crop in the spring, while rye was the principal winter crop. Rye could be grown in the poor soil common in the north, but it had low returns. Farmers in the central and southern regions grew more oats and wheat. Much of it was exported to European countries by the government, which sold the grain to offset part of the peasants' tax obligations. Peasants rarely earned more than about $150 a year, regardless of what type of work they did.

Most of the grain they raised went to feed peasant families, in the form of rye bread and buckwheat porridge. On average, peasants ate three pounds of bread a day, and more during harvest time. They also grew cabbages and cucumbers that could be stored in brine for the long winter months and root vegetables such as turnips and parsnips that could be stored in cold weather. Vegetables were the staple of their diet, especially during those weeks of the year when Russian church laws forbade people from consuming animal products, including milk and eggs. Peasants rarely had meat anyway. A popular peasant saying compared themselves with the nearby landowners: "We look at the same sky but eat a different dinner."

Peasants drank beverages made from fermented grains and, after the 1800s, tea. Observers noted that both male and female peasants enjoyed alcoholic beverages, and many became drunk at festive occasions.

To increase their income, a number of peasant families took on extra work, especially during the winter months when farming was impossible. Cottage industries, as they were called, often employed entire families. Many carved spoons or furniture from wood. They also produced jute rope, leather goods, pottery, metal objects, and cloth (usually from flax, a plant fiber used to make linen), or crafted religious objects, dolls, and toys. Peasants were paid per piece.

Scythe-wielding peasants head toward their work in the grain fields. Most of their crop returns went to pay the state's taxes.

Peasant families living under one roof included more than one generation. Parents lived with their unmarried or married sons and their sons' families, as well as any unmarried daughters. Their homes were unpainted log huts with thatch or shingle roofs and dirt floors. Moss was stuffed into the cracks to keep out the wind and rain. Most huts had only one room, but many also had a small entryway, as well as one or two storerooms. These were located below soil level or to the side of the hut. Storerooms held chickens and, occasionally, calves and lambs. Family members sometimes slept in upper-level storerooms during the warmer months. Sheds located near the huts held farm tools, carts, and machines.

Inside the houses were clay stoves, which might take up one-fourth of the interior space, measuring about five feet long and four feet wide. People, especially children and the elderly, slept atop the stove's flat surface on cold nights. Stoves also were used for cooking and providing warmth during the six long months of winter. A hole in the roof allowed smoke to escape.

Furnishings were simple benches and tables, blankets, and a few cooking utensils, which were placed on open shelves. Simple clothing hung on wall hooks. Pots of sunflowers and other blooms adorned peasant huts during the growing season.

Icons of saints were displayed in a corner of the main room of most huts. Upon entering the hut, people were expected to remain silent until they made the sign of the cross and bowed in the direction of the icon. Men had to remove their hats.

Peasant clothing was simple and sturdy. Men wore loose shirts over trousers, with a belt. Boots were made of felt or birch bark and frequently rose above calf level. Fur caps with earflaps and sheepskin coats and extra tunics were worn in the winter. Clothing could be vivid, especially clothes worn on Sundays and holidays. Women, especially in Siberia, often made their print skirts, aprons, bodices, and jackets from bright purples, greens, reds and pinks, tans, and browns. They tied back their hair with vibrant kerchiefs. People changed their clothing each week after taking a steam bath in the village bathhouse on Saturday afternoons. They rarely had soap for washing.

"Here All Is from God"

The peasants of Siberia, to the east of the Ural Mountains, had never been serfs and lived somewhat differently from peasants in the rest of Russia. An old saying in this region was, "Here all is from God and for the people."[6] These people settled the land on their own, as pioneers, serfs escaping bondage, fugitives, and ex-convicts. There had never been serf-owning landowners in Siberia, and Siberian peasants were usually more prosperous than other Russian peasants. Their huts often had brightly painted shutters and fancy, carved window frames.

Ukrainian peasants also had slightly different lifestyles. They built clay homes, whitewashed, with thatch roofs. Their homes were usually larger and cleaner than those in Great Russia. Ukrainian peasants enjoyed better farming conditions and a higher living standard than their counterparts in most of Russia.

Jews living in rural Russia had different traditions and problems. For centuries, they had been banned from owning land or farming and were forced to live in certain parts of Russia, mainly eastern Poland, Lithuania, and Ukraine. They became active in mining, the timber industry, shipping, and grain trade. In western Russia, rural and urban Jews were of-

"Slowly Starving to Death"

At the turn of the century, many observers described worsening conditions in rural Russia. Many people lacked adequate food and had to subsist on bread and water for weeks, even months, at a time. The hungry were not only poor farmers but many others who did not earn enough money. In 1877, the *Samara Gazette* reported the death of an eighteen-year-old village schoolteacher. Her monthly salary was 7½ rubles, and 3 rubles went to pay for her small rented room. She starved to death after school officials neglected to pay her for two months.

Poor harvests led to severe famines and mass starvation in 1891 and again in 1897. Yet, under Alexander III (1881–1894), Russia continued to export tons of grain. The Russian minister of finances declared, "We ourselves shall go without food, but we shall export." Of course, those who had to go without were the poor, not the minister himself or other members of the aristocracy.

In 1894, the *New York Tribune* reported:

> The truth is that the Russian peasant, all 100,000,000 of him, is . . . slowly starving to death. His diet consists of meal, flour and grits, cabbage and potatoes; no meat, except three times a year. His diet is insufficient, and less than in any civilized country. The hovel he lives in is two and a half yards long and one and one-half yards high, harboring the whole family and whatever cattle he possesses.

ten peddlers, traders, or artisans—cabinet-makers, tailors, cigar makers, and shoemakers.

Jews and Christians tended to live apart. Jews spoke a different language (Yiddish), and Jewish children were sent to Jewish schools. The hairstyles and clothing of Orthodox Jews further set them apart. Education levels among Jews were higher than among peasants throughout Russia, but laws limited their chances for higher education and certain jobs. Hoping for more civil rights and opportunities, about 1.25 million Jews emigrated from Russia between 1894 and 1924.

Community Life

Peasants in Great Russia shared land with other villagers. Livestock roamed on a communal grazing area. In Siberia, such areas could be several hundred acres large. A fence surrounded the village, and gates stood at the point of the fence where it crossed the road on each side of the village.

In the early 1900s, landowners and middle-class farmers organized larger farms and hired peasants to work for them at low wages. These people were called *kulaks*, which means "fist," and were often disliked and resented.

Currency was rare before the 1900s. People traded goods or bartered goods and services with others to obtain what they wanted. Fairs had nearly disappeared in Europe by the 1800s but were still common in Russia after 1900. In 1910, the summer Great Fair at Nizhni Novgorod, which lies at the junction of the Volga and Oka Rivers, drew four hundred thousand people. Traders offered metal goods, tea, goods from the Orient, furs, textiles, dried fish, books, and other items.

Peasant villages were organized so that local committees determined how land was distributed to residents. These communes were administered by elders elected by the peasants. Elders assigned strips of land to the heads of households. Peasants also shared forests and pasturelands. Elders made other decisions regarding farming and various neighborhood problems.

Among other things, the commune was required to gather the taxes that local authorities collected for the imperial treasury. Taxes remained high in the years leading up to the revolution. Of the 208 million rubles raised in taxes at the turn of the century, 195 million rubles came from the peasants.

Fragile Loyalty

For centuries, peasants viewed the czar as a distant father; they even nicknamed him *Batiushka-Czar*, meaning "father of the Russian people." Peasants were loyal to their image of the czar, who they believed would protect and help them as God's agent on earth. Many peasants thought that the czar wished for the peasants to have all the land but the landlords stood in his way.

The peasants tended to take out their resentments on the array of bureaucrats—landowners, local governors, government bureaucrats, and police—who stood between them and the imperial government. They complained bitterly about the government itself, since it represented heavy taxation and unwanted control over their lives, but were loyal to their czar.

Most peasants also observed the customs of the state-sponsored Russian Orthodox Church, which promised them happiness in heaven if they followed its teachings on earth.

One of the basic tenets of the church was that people should accept God's will and bear their earthly burdens stoically. A well-known saying among the peasants shows an ironic resignation toward their living conditions: "God is on high and the tsar a long way off."[7]

Historian Richard Pipes summarizes the attitude of a Russian peasant this way:

> He regarded the tsar as God's vicar on earth, a bolshak [father] of all Russia, created by the Lord to give him orders and to take care of him. He gave the tsar credit for all that was good and blamed whatever went wrong either on God's will or on the landlords and officials.[8]

Pipes and other historians explain that the people's loyalty toward their monarch was shallow. The desire of many peasant farmers, and other Russians, to change their way of life would exceed their allegiances to the czar. Pipes writes,

> Every Russian sought to extricate himself from the land: the peasant desired nothing better than to abandon the fields and become a pedlar, artisan, or usurer; the rural merchant, to join the nobility; the noble to move into the city or make a career in the state service.[9]

In the years leading up to the revolution, more peasants sought new lives in Russian cities. More became educated as the government built new rural schools. Education and urban life changed the attitudes of many peasants, who would unite with intellectuals and working-class Russians to revolutionize the nation.

Rich Man, Poor Man: Life in Russian Cities

At the time of the revolution, Russian cities had experienced four decades of rapid growth. The industrial revolution reached Russia in the late 1800s, decades later than in Europe and the United States. In 1854 there were only 9,944 industrial enterprises in Russia; by 1896, that number had quadrupled as more people moved from rural areas seeking jobs. By 1900, coal, oil, and iron ore production had tripled from 1854 figures.

New, larger railways were built to carry raw materials and manufactured goods. The fifteen-thousand-mile-long Trans-Siberian Railroad was completed in 1891. Linking Russia with China and Europe, it made it possible to transport goods over longer distances more quickly. During these years, more Russians came into contact with people from other countries. They were exposed to new ideas, both through travel and improved communication systems.

Trade and industry became more important to the Russian economy, especially after large deposits of iron and coal were found in

Russia in 1914

Arctic Ocean

Bering Sea

Norwegian Sea

North Sea

NL NORWAY

DK SWEDEN

GERMANY Baltic Sea FINLAND

Kara Sea

Warsaw

POLAND Vilna

Pinsk

Borodino

Moscow

St. Petersburg

Pechora River

Lena River

Sea of Okhotsk

AUSTRIA-HUNGARY

Kishinev Kiev

Odessa

R U S S I A N   E M P I R E

S I B E R I A

URAL MOUNTAINS

Dnieper River

Don River

Volga River

Lena River

Black Sea

CRIMEA

Orenburg Ekaterinburg

Stavropol

TRANS-SIBERIAN RAILROAD

Lake Baikal

MANCHURIA

Sea of Japan

OTTOMAN EMPIRE

Caspian Sea

Lake Aral KAZAKH Lake Balkhash

JAPAN

KOREA

CHINA

PERSIA

AFGHANISTAN

Yellow Sea

the Donets Basin of southwest Russia. Rich deposits of oil were found in Baku. Iron, salt, copper, textiles, papermaking, and glassmaking became the nation's largest industries. Banking and commerce grew, and foreign investors began financing development in Russia, a nation they had come to regard as "backward."

As industry grew, so did the number of professionals, merchants, and businessmen, which created a larger middle class. The working class also expanded after 1880, especially in cities like Moscow and St. Petersburg. The lives of workers and their families were quite different from those of middle-class and wealthy Russians who lived in these same cities. In one part of town, well-dressed people attended banquets and balls and filled seats at the theaters and imperial ballet. In other neighborhoods, people struggled to survive.

Upper-Class St. Petersburg

St. Petersburg was the seat of the administrative government in Russia and the official home of the imperial family. The city had a distinctive European look, largely because

Italian architects had designed most of the public buildings using baroque and Renaissance designs.

During the day, the streets were busy with coaches, carriages, horses, and streetcars as people went to and from their jobs or came to shop. By 1917, electric trams had greatly replaced horse-drawn carriages. Street vendors offered their wares—needles and thread, leather and knitted goods, pencils, shoelaces, hot tea, nuts, and different kinds of food. By the early 1900s, many new goods were being featured in the shops. They included imported bicycles, typewriters, cameras, and sewing machines.

At night, lighthearted Russians wearing splendid brocades, silks, velvets, furs, and jewels went to the ballet, Theatre Français, or elegant dress balls. Afterward, they might dine and dance at fashionable clubs. Red sleighs carried them across the icy streets during the long, dark winters.

For high society, the official social season began on New Year's Day. For the next few months, affluent Russians hosted and attended balls, banquets, concerts, and after-theater suppers. The ball held by the royal couple at the Winter Palace on New Year's

St. Petersburg was the administrative capital of Russia. A trade center with a cosmopolitan air, St. Petersburg offered economic opportunities and social amenities unknown to Russia's peasant population.

Upper- and middle-class Russians living in St. Petersburg were known to throw lavish balls in their luxurious homes.

Day was the most important event. Guests included the Russian diplomatic corps and members of the upper four levels of the civil service, along with important military personnel. A noblewoman who attended these balls later described the scene as guests arrived:

> Carriages arriving in an unbroken line. Open sledges bringing those officers who did not fear the cold; the horses' harness covered with blue netting to prevent accumulations of snow from being blown into the passengers' faces. . . . The guests went up the grand staircases of white marble, on the soft velvety carpets; white and scarlet uniforms; spreadeagle helmets in gold and silver; countless epaulets . . . white dolmans bordered with precious beaver fur; finally, the court uniforms, heavy with gold embroidery and completed by short breeches and white silk stockings.[10]

Upper- and middle-class Russians lived in the central part of St. Petersburg, where luxurious homes lined exclusive streets. These houses were often palatial, designed by Italian architects and built in ornate rococo and neoclassical styles. Nearby were impressive buildings that housed the Royal Mariinski Theater, where ballet and opera were performed. At the Royal Alexandrinsky Theater, outstanding actors performed dramas and comedies written by Russians and foreign writers.

Wealthy noble families supported their lifestyles with the rent from their estates or the sale of large tracts of land. They could afford spacious homes filled with Persian carpets, fine furniture, grand pianos, and works of art. There was plenty of food and drink, often shared with guests and visitors. Expensive meats, champagne, tropical fruits, and other tempting foods graced their dinner tables, along with elegant flowers. Flowers that were not grown in hothouses were often imported from other countries or brought in from the Crimea during the winter.

The wealthiest families had hundreds of servants to tend to their homes and children and to provide entertainment at banquets and balls. Some servants had jobs so specific that they were required only to fill water glasses at the dining table or light their master's pipe. Often, wealthy Russians traveled with large groups of servants and train cars full of belongings to elegant resorts and spas or gambling casinos in Europe. These tourists were often among the most flamboyant people at such resorts.

Children from well-to-do families received the best education. They were sometimes tutored at home during the early years and could attend select secondary schools. Many of the top schools, such as the Nicholas Engineering School, were military academies. Wealthy young men ten and older might

Exquisite Jewels

Russian women were known as jewelry lovers and enjoyed the chance to wear their finest gems. World-famous jewelers had establishments in St. Petersburg and Moscow. Outstanding craftsmen working in these cities and workshops elsewhere in Russia created their fabulous wares.

The famous ballerina Mathilde Kschessinskaya, who was married to a member of the royal family, was the proud owner of many precious objects. She described the display she arranged for guests at a dinner party she hosted in 1917, the year of the revolution.

> I brought out countless trinkets and works of art which had been stored since the beginning of the war (among other things there was a superb collection of artificial flowers made of precious stones and a small gold fir tree, with branches shimmering with little diamonds). There were so many of these things that I complained to my sister that I had not enough room to display them.

One of the most famous jewelry establishments was the house of Fabergé, renowned as the official court jeweler. Fabergé became world famous for its creations, especially fabulous jewel-encrusted eggs. Author Harrison E. Salisbury describes the work done there:

Skilled artists created magical baubles —sapphire cornflowers, ruby scarletinas, pearl-and-emerald lilies-of-the-valley, nosegays of precious stones whose sparkle blinded the viewer. Their supreme achievements, the Easter "surprises," were invented for the Imperial family. Each Easter, the Czar (beginning with Alexander III and continuing through Nicholas II) presented a Fabergé egg to his wife. Such an egg! It might encase a miniature brood of chicks. Or it might harbor within an intricate gold and enamel shell a working replica of the Trans-Siberian railroad.

This Fabergé egg is covered with a ribbon of diamonds. Such ornate trinkets were coveted by the upper classes as displays of wealth.

attend the Emperor Alexander Lyceum, His Imperial Majesty's Corps of Pages, which was located in St. Petersburg's Vorontsov Palace, or the Imperial Law College. Students at these schools wore military-style uniforms. After graduation, they had to serve for at least three years in some government post.

Boarding schools for girls, called institutes, accepted students from the gentry or urban middle classes. The most prestigious institutes, founded by Russian empresses, included the Smolny and Catherine Institutes in St. Petersburg. A typical uniform for female students consisted of a white cape and apron worn over a darker dress, a frilled bonnet, and white gloves.

The Growing Middle Classes

A small number of Russians belonged to the middle class, called bourgeoisie in some countries. They could afford to live comfortably and educate their children well. Some had enough money to travel and to attend universities. Most lived in the cities, and many had summer homes or estates. Their money had either been inherited or earned through successful trade and businesses.

Industrialization increased the number of Russian merchants, who retained the classification of merchant regardless of their wealth. Among the richest of these men was multimillionaire Timofey Morozov, who made his fortune in banking, textiles, and railways. Another member of the merchant estate, Mikhail Korolyov, was the mayor of Moscow in the years leading up to the revolution.

Like other Russians, wealthy merchant families were known for their hospitality. In

The bourgeoisie of Russia lived comfortable lives. Many could afford to travel, send their children to college, and entertain in their homes.

Siberia, when merchants entertained guests at a party, it was considered impolite if any inch of the tablecloth could be seen after food and drinks were placed on the table.

Some prominent financiers, shipping magnates, industrialists, and merchants were Jewish. At the time of the revolution, there were about 7 million Jews in Russia. Despite laws that discriminated against them, Jews managed to develop strong communities and contributed a great deal to art, music, and literature, as well as to Russia's education system and economic development. Some built successful businesses, such as breweries, flour mills, textile mills, and tobacco factories. Although some individuals were able to become wealthy, most Jews remained poor whether they lived in cities or rural areas.

Thriving Culture

In the years preceding the revolution, industrialists, middle-class Russians, and some nobles made significant contributions to cultural life in Russia. They provided both talent and support for music, drama, literature, and art.

Like other areas of Russian life, these were dominated by the state. Art, for example, was controlled and financed by the government. At the Russian Academy of Art, where an artist could receive free training, the state chose who would be admitted. The government chose the faculty and specified which styles of art, namely traditional, were acceptable. The government was also the main purchaser of artwork.

Things changed with the growth of the wealthy merchant class. The Morozov family made significant contributions to the Moscow Art Theatre and various art galleries, in addition to patronizing promising individual artists. The Tereshchencko family of Kiev, whose wealth came from the sugar trade, sponsored artists and musicians. Industrialists and their children amassed important collections of art, books, sculpture, manuscripts, and furniture. They exposed Russian artists to the new styles that were being developed in other countries such as France and Germany.

Russian artists also began experimenting with new styles and subject matter. Some realistically portrayed the lives of ordinary Russians and scenes of modern industrial life.

Moscow: "The Third Rome"

Moscow, sometimes called the Third Rome, lay in the center of Russia and formed a meeting place for railroads, waterways, and thus, trade. This was the ancient capital of Russia. Standing in its center was the Kremlin, virtually a city in itself. This imposing complex with its distinctive red walls had been built in medieval times. A Frenchman who visited the Kremlin in the 1900s described it this way:

> This curious conglomeration of palaces, towers, churches, monasteries, chapels, barracks, arsenals and bastions; this incoherent jumble of sacred and secular buildings; this complex of functions as fortress, sanctuary, seraglio [palace], harem, necropolis, and orison [place of worship]; this blend of advanced civilization and archaic barbarism; this violent conflict of crudest materialism and most lofty spirituality; are they not the whole history of Russia, the whole epic of the Russian nation, the whole inward drama of the Russian soul?

Others painted in the cubist and expressionist styles that were popular throughout Europe during the early 1900s.

During these years, Anton Chekhov produced short stories and innovative plays that would become world classics. Shalom Aleichem wrote his famed collection of Yiddish short stories in Kiev, while novelist Maksim Gorky wrote his famous play *The Lower Depths*. Russian poets and philosophers gained world acclaim, as did artists such as the expressionist painter Wassily Kandinsky.

The Russian ballet was also unsurpassed. Choreographer Marius Petipa dazzled the world with productions that featured world-famous Russian ballet dancers, including Tamara Karsavina and the immortal Anna Pavlova. Producer Sergey Diaghilev teamed with a French choreographer, Michel Fokine, to create the Ballet Russe.

Equally prominent and influential were Russian composers—Nikolay Rimsky-Korsakov, Sergey Rachmaninoff, Igor Stravinsky, and Sergey Prokofiev. Outstanding violinists, pianists, and other instrumentalists trained in Russia performed around the world.

The People's Palace

A few Russians could afford the best seats and boxes in the finest theaters and concert halls. For less affluent people in St. Petersburg, Nicholas II built the People's Palace in 1901. For a small fee (twenty kopecks), people could attend concerts, plays, and ballet performances, seeing performances that equaled those at the expensive facilities. Many upperclass Russians also went to the People's Palace. For the poorest Russians in the city, saving even twenty kopecks from their wages was difficult.

The work of Russian dramatist, short story writer, and novelist Anton Chekhov is studied today as classic literature.

As industry expanded, working-class neighborhoods grew in large cities, as well as in industrial centers outside the cities. Living conditions and wages depended greatly on where and for whom people worked. For example, workers at the steel and arms factory in Izhevsk were assigned to individual timber houses with small garden plots. This was quite unusual, however. Most workers toiled long hours for low wages and lived in overcrowded, unsanitary housing.

Factory workers lived and worked in the outer parts of the cities where factories were located. Many of the larger factories built barren tenements, similar to military barracks, to house their workers. The ground floor of these buildings held a kitchen and dining hall. On the upper floors were dormitory rooms, divided up for single men, married couples, women with children, and families. In some barracks, families shared small rooms with other people and took turns sleeping in the beds or on the floor.

Workers in smaller factories had to find their own housing. Grim city tenement apart-ments stood on unpaved back streets without city lights or sewer systems. Rooms lacked running water and toilet facilities.

Those who could not afford an apartment had to stay in the factory day and night. After a grueling workday that often lasted twelve, or even eighteen, hours, these workers and their families ate their evening meal in the factory and slept on the workshop floors. This arrangement was most prevalent in Moscow, where 60 percent of the workers "lived" around the clock in their workplaces.

New laws passed in 1903 and 1906 gave workers more rights and benefits. Free medical care and pensions were made available to workers who were injured on the job or became too sick to work. Trade unions were legalized in 1906 but were subject to numerous restrictions. Many employers chose to ignore these laws, and enforcement was weak.

Observers said that drinking was a common escape for workers grappling with life in the competitive, crowded slums. Vodka was a

Alcohol consumption provided an escape for workers who often lived in shabby conditions. This man lived in a Workers' Hostel, probably near a factory where he toiled long hours during the day.

Russian workers banded together in the late nineteenth century to protest unfair working conditions. The few concessions they received led to the widespread outrage that culminated in the 1917 revolution.

popular drink—although many could only afford it on special occasions—as were wine and beer. The government controlled the sale of vodka and reaped the profits. Gambling was also common.

People struggled to survive, day by day and week by week. A critic of the czarist system, nineteenth-century Russian author Leo Tolstoy, said, "All our palaces, all our theaters, museums, all this stuff, these riches of ours we owe to the effort of these same hungry people who make these things. This means that they will always be obliged to do this kind of work to save themselves from the death by starvation that constantly hangs over their heads."[11]

Labor Struggles

Workers began to form labor groups in the 1870s. In St. Petersburg, labor clubs and workers' circles gradually attracted hundreds, then thousands, of members. These groups discussed their common problems and goals. They wanted better working conditions, higher wages, and shorter workdays.

At times, workers went on strike to get action from their employers. The first reported labor strike in Russia occurred outside Moscow in 1885. Eight thousand textile workers took part, but they were quashed at once by czarist police. A newspaper article attributed the strike to "revolutionary propaganda" from western Europe.

Workers became more numerous and more vocal, and they refused to give up their struggle. In 1886, thirty thousand workers remained on strike for four weeks. More than one thousand of these men were arrested, but this strike inspired others, and strikes continued to occur regularly.

The government made some concessions. In 1897, the workday was officially reduced to 11½ hours for adults and 9 hours a day for children. Sunday was designated as a nonworking day. Earlier laws had banned the hiring of children younger than twelve and had limited children's workdays to eight hours. However, employers, including the government, Russia's largest employer, frequently broke these laws. Inspectors charged with enforcing labor laws often ignored offenders and accepted bribes to keep quiet.

Year after year, workers again presented their demands and received little in response. Their resentment and pent-up frustration would fuel a major rebellion in 1905 and the Russian Revolution of 1917.

An Iron Hand: Czarism and the Imperial Family

When he became czar in 1894, Nicholas II referred to his new role as "that awful job I have feared all my life."[12] Since his earliest years, Nicholas had known he would rule someday, in the autocratic tradition of his ancestors. However, this new czar—a shy, family-centered outdoorsman with no gift for politics—would prove to be a weak leader during turbulent times.

Each czar had interpreted his role somewhat differently. Some imposed strict control over their subjects; others sought to compromise, giving people more freedom and control over their lives. There had been reoccurring acts of rebellion by the people and suppression by the government. Terrorism against the regime was also an ongoing threat.

Terrorism and Repression

Only thirty-five years before Nicholas took the throne, his grandfather, Alexander II, had freed the serfs and enacted other reforms. Alexander II, the "Czar-Liberator," authorized a system of local rural councils, elected by the people, with limited powers of self-rule. New roads, hospitals, and schools were built.

To improve the criminal justice system, trial by jury was introduced, and punishments for small crimes were reduced. Peasants were allowed to choose their own mates, buy and sell property, and institute legal proceedings in court. The czar also changed old laws that required peasants to serve up to twenty-five years in the military, although some service was still required.

Alexander II might have thought people would applaud his efforts. Instead, there was increasing rebellion, and his life was often threatened.

A small minority of Russians, primarily university professors and students, wanted more radical change, including an end to imperial rule. However, the peasants seemed indifferent to their cause and most middle-class Russians shied away from politics. Some of these frustrated revolutionaries formed terrorist groups.

Among these groups were Young Russia, Land and Freedom, and the People's Will. Terrorists used two major approaches: violence to shock and unite people in their anger toward the government, and a combination of education and propaganda. Revolutionaries would continue to use these different methods in the years that followed. The Executive Committee of the People's Will stated its goal:

> Terrorist activity has as its objective undermining the fascination with the government's might, providing an uninterrupted demonstration of the possibility of struggling against the government, in this manner lifting the revolutionary spirit of the people and its faith in the success of its cause, and, finally, organizing the forces capable of combat.[13]

On March 1, 1881, a young member of this group flung a bomb at the czar's carriage as it moved along a St. Petersburg street. The bomb exploded and caused ghastly injuries that resulted in the death of Alexander II that same day. As his attendants bent over his shattered, bloody body, they heard him say, "To the palace, to die there."[14] The bomb also killed a boy who was watching the procession and a Cossack guard. Young Nicholas was at the palace when his grandfather's body was brought back.

The new czar, Nicholas's father, Alexander III, ruled more strictly. He halted plans Alexander II had made to set up a representative council to consult with the czar on national issues. Alexander III also enlarged his police force, which was ordered to vigorously fight terrorism. Police were given new powers to halt public and private gatherings and to arrest and punish people suspected of antigovernment actions.

Later, A. A. Lopukhin, who headed the Department of Police from 1902 to 1905, strongly criticized these decrees. He said that they caused the "entire population of Russia to become dependent on the personal opinions of the functionaries of political police." Lopukhin had little hope for the longevity of the imperial government. He concluded that the czarist police "constitute the entire might of a regime whose existence has come to an end."[15] Other critics pointed out that even in the worst year for terrorism (1880), the police found relatively few incidents—fewer than one thousand among a population of 100 million.

Further Restrictions

Starting in the 1880s, Russians were subjected to new restrictions. Among other things, no one could start a newspaper, open

Alexander III ruled Russia more strictly than his predecessor and gave no leniency to citizens suspected of terrorism or antigovernment sentiment.

any school, give a charity concert, sell newspapers on the street, change their place of business, or travel more than fifteen miles from home without first obtaining permission from a government official. The Criminal Code of 1885 listed new laws meant to protect the "sacred person," the dignity, and the supreme authority of the czar. Under these laws, the penalties for harming a statue or portrait of the czar or portraying him in an irreverent way were more severe than assaulting or even killing another person.

Although his own life was threatened several times, Alexander III died a natural death from a bronchial infection at age forty-nine. As the oldest male in his family of five, twenty-six-year-old Nicholas was czarevitch—next in line to the throne. Following family tradition, he said, "I shall maintain the principle of autocracy just as firmly and unflinchingly as it was preserved by my unforgettable dead father."[16]

Under the czar were the bureaucracy, the army, and the church, each with its tightly organized hierarchy of officials. Education was also strongly tied to the bureaucracy. When the first Russian universities were set up in 1804, one of their main functions was to prepare people for government service.

The Russian Orthodox Church played an important role in Russian society. The church had been made part of the state by Peter the Great, who became czar in 1682. By 1700, the church was a branch of the government, overseen by the czar's lieutenants. Ordained priests took an oath in which they vowed "to defend unsparingly all the powers, rights and prerogatives belonging to the High Autocracy of his Majesty."[17]

Strict laws forbade people from leaving the church or trying to win converts for any other religion. About two-thirds of the people in the Russian Empire considered themselves members. This included nearly all ethnic Russians, since other residents of the empire were Turks and Tartars in Central Asia, Finns, Estonians, Poles, Latvians, Germans, and Mongols, all of whom traditionally followed other religions.

With their tall spires and gilded domes, grand Orthodox churches were the pride of the nation. More than four hundred stood in Moscow alone, which was called the City of

Anti-Semitism in Imperial Russia

Under most czars, religions other than the Orthodox Church were either barely tolerated or not accepted at all. Anti-Semitism was prevalent during the late 1800s and early 1900s, at which time about half of the world's Jews lived within the borders of the Russian Empire. Practicing Jews who lived in Russia did not enjoy the same civil rights as others. Most were forbidden to farm. They could not become civil servants or rise to the rank of an officer in the army. Intermarriage between Jews and Christians was forbidden.

Jews who changed their religion—converted—to the Orthodox Church were permitted all the rights enjoyed by Christians in Russia. However, converting meant antagonizing one's community and family and going against tradition. Thus there were few religious converts in czarist Russia.

In many areas, Jews were harassed and subjected to pogroms—physical attacks on their lives and property. As villagers attacked Jews, law enforcement officials stood by without stopping the violence. At times, the government initiated such attacks during times of political unrest. Officials thought they could redirect people's anger at the czar to another group, in this case Jews, who would serve as scapegoats.

Margarita Zarudny, a non-Jew, recalled the pogroms that took place during the early 1900s in her rural village. During one pogrom, her father, an engineer, tried to protect some Jewish families. In *Russia Speaks: An Oral History from the Revolution*, by Richard Lourie, Zarudny recalled, "He was beaten up by the mob *and* arrested by the police. Both! He spent three months in solitary confinement until finally his connections in the capital helped him get out."

Many idealistic Jews became active in revolutionary activities. They hoped for a more just society in which religious persecution would be illegal and people of all faiths would work together for the common good.

Forty Times Forty Churches. The more humble stone churches and wooden chapels in the countryside often were well designed and housed sacred art objects. Atop these buildings were the distinctive onion-shaped domes, usually painted blue or green.

Inside, large churches and cathedrals glittered with candles, icons, and statues. Bearded clergy officiated in gold-trimmed, bejeweled robes and headpieces. Liturgical music inspired strong emotions, especially during holidays, particularly Easter. Church choirs tried to outperform one another.

Religious Traditions

Religious traditions were an integral part of life for both rural and urban Russians. These traditions began at birth with baptism, at which time infants received a cross to be worn around the neck from that day on. The church calendar governed people's schedules as they attended mass and took part in fasts, festivals, feast days, and holy days.

With its rules and rituals, the church helped to maintain the status quo—the existing state of affairs. Church leaders told their congregations they must not challenge or disobey the divine authority of their rulers. Church teachings and traditions stressed patriotism, and the czar often appeared alongside church leaders for important ceremonies or annual holidays and events. A major Orthodox principle was that people should accept their fate as the will of God. Along with this, their faith urged people to be humble.

As in other areas of Russian life, the czar had the last word. Church leaders could be stripped of their titles and functions if they displeased him. For instance, during his reign, Nicholas II exiled a bishop who disagreed with his decision to canonize (declare

as a saint) a Russian monk who had died years earlier.

Historians have debated how deeply religious most Russians were before the revolution. Russians attended services and followed religious traditions, but some observers view these acts as superficial, reflecting a desire to reach heaven after death rather than growing out of deep spiritual convictions. Many, especially peasants, were superstitious and could be influenced by the wandering, self-appointed holy men and healers who traveled around the country offering prayers and prophecies in exchange for economic support. In cities, sophisticated Russians often ignored moral dictates of the church and discussed new philosophical ideas.

The grandeur of churches such as St. Basil's in Moscow emphasized the importance of religion in Russian life.

During the reign of Nicholas II, many Russian intellectuals rejected the church in favor of atheism, which rejects the idea of any supreme, supernatural being. Intellectuals also decried the partnership between the church and the autocracy. These sentiments would later advance the Bolshevik goal of eliminating religion from Russian life.

As he accepted the idea of autocracy, so did Czar Nicholas II follow church traditions. It was the life he had been born into. The last czar understood little about the everyday lives of his subjects, much less the new, and often radical, religious, political, and economic movements that were taking hold. His own upbringing had been far removed from the world outside the imperial palace.

Future czar Nicholas Romanov, here pictured at age six. Nicholas led a life of luxury and spent his early years learning languages and participating in outdoor sports like hunting and sailing.

Born to Rule

Nicholas Romanov was born in 1868, one of five children. He and his siblings lived in a nine-hundred-room palace and spent time in other palaces and large vacation homes, surrounded by great luxury. Yet, the Romanov children were raised strictly and rather simply. Each morning, Nicholas rose early, took a cold bath, and began his academic lessons. Among other things, he studied languages and became adept at English, French, and German. After a minimal lunch, the future czar spent hours learning horseback riding and military drill, as well as hunting, sailing, and ice-skating. He spent hours outdoors and enjoyed vigorous physical activities all his life.

As a young man, Nicholas enjoyed dining with friends and attended balls, concerts, and performances at the opera, theater, and ballet. At age nineteen, he spent several months commanding a squadron of the Horse Guard. He described the experience in letters to his mother:

Every day I become more and more used to camp life. Each day, we drill twice—there is either target practice in the morning and battalion drill in the evening or the other way round. . . . We have lunch at 12 o'clock and dine at 8, with siesta and tea in between. The dinners are very merry; they feed us well. After meals, the officers . . . play billiards, skittles, cards, or dominoes.[18]

When he was twenty-one, Nicholas fell in love with Princess Alix of Hesse-Darmstadt, a province in Germany. Her maternal grandmother was Queen Victoria of Great Britain, and Alix spent most of her youth in London at Kensington Palace after her mother died when she was just six years old. Nicholas met Alix when, as a twelve-year-old, she came to St. Petersburg for the wedding of her sister Ella to Grand Duke Sergey, the younger brother of Czar Alexander III. Their romance began five years later when Alix visited her sister in St. Petersburg during the winter.

In 1892, the affectionate, sensitive Nicholas wrote in his diary of his determination to make twenty-year-old Alix Victoria Helena Louise Beatrice, princess of Hesse-Darmstadt, his bride: "My dream is some day to marry Alix H. I have loved her a long while and still deeper and stronger since 1889 when she spent six weeks in St. Petersburg."[19]

At first, the prospect of marriage seemed remote. To marry the heir to the throne, Alix had to accept the Russian Orthodox faith. However, she was a staunch Lutheran and did not want to change her religion. But Nicholas was persistent, and as the two were deeply in love, Alix finally agreed to become his wife. Conscientiously, the princess, who took the Russian name Alexandra, began studying her new religion and the Russian language.

The Last Coronation

During this otherwise joyful time, Nicholas lost his father. He expressed deep concerns to close family members, telling them he was unprepared and loath to become czar. Nicholas wrote in his diary, "I know absolutely nothing about matters of state. I have not the least idea of how to address my ministers."[20]

After the traditional mourning ceremonies and a state funeral, Alexander III was buried on November 19. One week later, Nicholas and Alexandra married in a simple ceremony at the Winter Palace. The bride wore a traditional Russian court robe of white and silver and received the diamond nuptial crown from her mother-in-law, the popular Empress Marie. Large crowds cheered the royal couple as they left the palace. Because the nation was still in mourning, there was no reception or honeymoon.

On May 26, 1896, Nicholas and Alexandra were officially crowned emperor and em-

In November 1895 Nicholas married Princess Alix of Hesse-Darmstadt, the granddaughter of Queen Victoria. The two were crowned emperor and empress of Russia in May 1896.

press. The Russian monarchy claimed to be all-powerful and appointed by God. The religious rites, prayers, hymns, and pomp of the occasion reflected these ideas. The ceremony took place in the ancient capital, Moscow, not the newer and more westernized St. Petersburg. Tens of thousands of Russians gathered for this special occasion, which included a three-day break from work and much pageantry and feasting.

A long, formal procession of uniformed men preceded Nicholas and Alexandra to the Ouspensky Cathedral. Soldiers in the Imperial Guard, dressed in gold, red, and white, flanked the long, velvet-covered staircase that led inside. Priests led the Romanovs down the staircase into the glowing, candlelit cathedral with its five gilded cupolas. The couple then sat before the altar on chairs studded with hundreds of radiant diamonds and other gems. Before them stood the highest-ranking clergy in the nation, dressed in traditional

Coronation Day Tragedy

Born on the day the Russian calendar assigned to Job, a biblical character who endured many hardships, Nicholas often expressed a wry, fatalistic attitude about life. Various events seemed to him bad omens, meant to confirm his feelings of dread. For instance, at his coronation, an important ceremonial symbol worn by czars

Nicholas and Alexandra ride through the streets on their way to their coronation. The event drew tremendous crowds, and hundreds of Russian citizens would die in a public stampede for souvenirs the following day.

during this ceremony fell from his shoulders and hit the floor.

Far worse was the tragedy that occurred the day after the coronation. A huge crowd of five hundred thousand people had come to Moscow for the traditional open-air feast that would be held in a field outside the city. Free beer would be distributed, along with small souvenirs, mostly enameled cups stamped with the imperial seal. As the crowds gathered in the night and morning, many began drinking. A rumor spread that there were not enough gifts and beverages to go around, which set off a stampede of people. The small group of Cossacks on the scene could not maintain order. Hundreds of people were trampled to death, and thousands of others were injured.

The czar and czarina were upset and told their family they would go to pray at a monastery to mourn the event. Instead, the czar's uncles insisted that he attend a lavish coronation ball being given for him by the French embassy. That night, the couple was subdued. The British ambassador reported to Queen Victoria, "The Empress appeared in great distress, her eyes reddened by tears."

The czar and czarina later visited injured people at hospitals and arranged for individual burials. They used personal funds to send money to each of the bereaved families. Nonetheless, they were harshly criticized for having attended a ball after such a tragedy. As a "foreigner," Alexandra came in for special rebuke. The new czar's reign thus began on a sore note.

robes and headpieces trimmed with diamonds, rubies, sapphires, and pearls. The ceremony itself lasted five hours. At the end, crowds cheered as the new czar and czarina bowed to them from the Red Stairway outside the church.

Palaces and Yachts

As monarchs of the richest kingdom on earth, the royal couple had at their disposal a variety of palatial estates and vacation homes, royal yachts, fabulous furnishings and jewels, and thousands of servants.

The Winter Palace, primary home of the royal family, covered three city blocks. Its

The only son of Nicholas II, Alexis suffered from hemophilia and was thus unable to partake in the same robust physical lifestyle that his father had enjoyed as a child.

enormous interior contained grand, white marble staircases lined with velvet carpets, and large columns made of marble and malachite went from the floor to the gilded ceilings, dotted with crystal and gold chandeliers. Five balls were held here for the nobility during the social season. A midnight supper at the palace might feature lobster, chicken, tarts and other pastries, wines and champagne.

The reserved Nicholas and Alexandra preferred a quiet family life to large social affairs. They enjoyed spending time at Tsarskoe Selo—the czar's village—located outside St. Petersburg. Here, Cossacks guarded the large Imperial Park, and numerous workers tended the velvety green lawns, man-made lakes, stone terraces, and fragrant gardens. There were two imposing residences, the blue-and-white, Italian-style, two-hundred-room palace built by Catherine the Great and the slightly smaller (one-hundred-room) Alexander Palace. Here, the czar and czarina made their primary home in one wing. For their growing family, they decorated several apartments in the style of an English country estate.

Family Life

Only a few outsiders were allowed to spend much time around the royal family. People who saw them close up remarked on their strong affection. For Nicholas and Alexandra, their children and family life brought great joy as well as great heartache.

After her marriage, the empress gave birth to four daughters. The couple was thrilled when their next child was a son, and therefore heir to the throne—Alexis, born in 1904. When he was scarcely a year old, it became apparent that Alexis was not well. He was diagnosed with hemophilia, an incurable and often painful illness in which blood does

Cotton, Not Silk

People imagined the czar and his family were extremely wealthy, but they were often short of cash, especially near the end of the year. Every New Year's Day, a fixed amount of money—more than 200 million rubles—was deposited into an account for the czar called the "privy Purse." A portion of this was for his personal use, but most was distributed as allowances to the many members of the Romanov family. The money also had to maintain the various palaces in St. Petersburg and its outskirts, in Moscow, and in the Crimea, and support the staffs of these places, which included more than fifteen thousand people. These same funds maintained three theaters in St. Petersburg and two in Moscow, the Academy of Arts, four art galleries, and the Imperial Ballet School.

For their personal use, Nicholas and Alexandra were left with about forty thousand pounds a year, some of which they gave to charities. This was far less than the annual amount allotted to British monarchs, for example. In their personal lives, the czar and czarina did not live as lavishly as their wealthier subjects. They often ate inexpensive foods, such as porridge, borscht, barley, and apple pudding. Nicholas was known to joke about wearing cotton socks instead of silk ones. He once told a naval officer, "Mine are cotton and they do get darned sometimes. There is so much to do with the money—I can't afford luxuries."

---

not clot properly. The disease is hereditary and is carried in the mother's genes. Certain injuries can cause death at any time.

Alexandra was plagued with grief and a sense of guilt, as well as continuing worry over her son's health. Frequently, Alexandra remained at her child's side day and night. She seemed withdrawn, nervous, and reluctant to appear in public.

This aggravated problems she already had with her husband's family and with the public. People criticized the czarina for not sending more social invitations and for entertaining so infrequently. Few people knew about the czarevitch's illness and the strain it was causing Alexandra. Some mistook her shyness and introverted nature for arrogance and unfriendliness.

The royal children also lived apart from ordinary Russians, and they spent most of their time with each other. They played outdoors, read, did needlework, played the piano, and studied. The family continued the tradition of each child taking a cold bath each morning. At age eight, the royal children—Grand Duchess Olga, Grand Duchess Tatiana, Grand Duchess Marie, Grand Duchess Anastasia, and Alexis—began serious studies with an English tutor, Charles Sydney Gibbes. They learned languages, including English, French, and German, as well as history and mathematics.

Alexis, who needed to be protected from bruising and cuts, had to avoid many physical activities. Onboard the royal yacht, he enjoyed playing with a red-and-blue kite, shuttlecock, deck billiards, and blowing bubbles with a set of straws. At times, the boy appeared rosy and healthy and lived a fairly normal life. Then, disaster would strike as he fell or bruised himself and began to bleed internally, causing him great pain. These episodes terrified his parents and absorbed time and energy Nicholas could have used to cope with

Imperial Isolation

Although the Romanovs enjoyed tremendous power and privilege, they were also hemmed in by constant guarding and tradition. Tight security surrounded the czar and his family. Even at Tsarskoe Selo, Cossack guards and other soldiers could be found inside and outside the family's residence, always ready to defend them from attack.

In 1894, as Alexander III lay dying, an editorial in the *New York Tribune* described the lack of peace of mind and the limited freedom of the czar:

> The career of Alexander III has been a melancholy illustration for the irony of a despot's fate. He was condemned to live in daily dread of the secret bullet and the exploding bomb. The most powerful of monarchs, he could not return through the Great Morskaia Prospect from the requiem service in honor of his father's memory without being a target for assassins; nor is he free to visit his capital unless an army is put in motion to protect him; nor can he make the rounds of his apartments in his secluded palace fortress without having detectives dogging his steps.

This carefully guarded way of life increased the isolation of the czar and kept him from grasping the mood of the country and urgent concerns of his people.

an increasingly unstable empire. Desperate for help for their son, the czar and czarina would also turn to disreputable spiritual healers, with disastrous results.

Reluctant Leader

By 1905, Nicholas II felt more secure in his position and less inclined to follow the orders of his older uncles. He approached his duties in the same conscientious way he had carried out responsibilities all his life, yet he remained a reluctant leader. The czar, viewed by most people as kind and well-meaning, was regarded as an indecisive person who disliked controversy and matters of state.

For her part, Alexandra preferred to stay at home more often, avoiding ceremonies, parties, and other public events. She spent time with close friends and in prayer or religious studies. Alexandra came to view the nobility and those who criticized her and her husband as aberrations, while the "real Russians," including the masses of peasants, were their true subjects—loyal and religious. As both she and Nicholas mingled even less with people, they were ill informed about life in the outside world.

At this turning point, Russia could have benefited from a leader who was strong, progressive, and involved. Nicholas lacked these qualities, and he did not have the ability to select ministers who could help him cope with rising discontent and revolutionary zeal. Devoted to his more strong-willed wife, he often chose to take her advice, even when his ministers disagreed. The temperament, isolation, and personal life of this czar would have a huge impact on the revolution.

"The Czar Will Not Help Us"

By 1905, Russia was on the brink of massive change. Revolutionary parties were steadily gaining members. Middle-class Russians with a strong sense of justice continued to call for political and economic reforms. There were rumblings of discontent in the countryside as peasants demanded more land and relief from famine.

Among the most vocal Russians were the intellectuals, students as well as professors. Groups met secretly to discuss ways to reform or abolish the czarist system. They were inspired by the successful revolutions that had taken place in France and other countries. It was in France, more than a century earlier, that a group of Russians had been moved to take action. The Decembrists, regarded as the first revolutionaries, became heroes to those who now yearned for a new Russia.

Early Revolts

Russian aristocrats who served as military officers in the Napoleonic Wars in 1812 and 1813 were exposed to new ideas about human rights and industrial progress. They began to see the plight of the peasants in a new light. Some adopted the idea of noblesse oblige—the idea that the privileged classes should help their poorer countrymen to a better life. Under their leadership, secret revolutionary groups were formed in Russia. Among them were the Union of Welfare, the Southern Society, and the Order of the Russian Knights,

which called for a more representative government and a constitution.

Some were willing to risk their lives. The first organized revolt in Russia took place in December 1825 as a new czar, Nicholas I, was crowned. Led by Pavel Pestel, thirty officers and three thousand soldiers set out to prevent the senators from taking their traditional oath of loyalty to the czar. However, Pestel's group failed to convince enough fellow soldiers to join them. Dozens of rebels were shot by soldiers who sided with the government.

Crowned czar of Russia in 1825, Nicholas I began his reign during a period of revolt, when the Russian people began to seek a government more representative of their interests.

Afterward, Pestel and other leaders were publicly hanged. This event became known as the Decembrist Uprising.

Nicholas I believed rebellion should be met by a strong show of force. More police were sent to patrol the streets and ferret out revolutionaries. Revolutionaries were not numerous or powerful enough to act under these conditions. However, they continued to meet and to communicate through their writings. For several decades, there would be periodic uprisings and skirmishes between these changing groups of revolutionaries and officials.

Universities became the hub of revolutionary discussions. By the mid-1800s, young people at universities were calling for reform. They wanted a more democratic form of government and economic reforms, including more land for peasants. Many revolutionaries came from middle-class or upper-middle-class families, though others came from poorer homes. As time went on, they decided that changing people's attitudes through education was the best way to promote change.

"Go to the People"

Populism gained support near the end of the 1800s. The populists, mostly middle-class urban intellectuals, believed that Russia should be governed by elected representatives. They hoped that peasants, who were by far the largest group in Russia, would demand an end to autocracy and more rights and a larger share of wealth for themselves. Dressed as peasants, they went to the countryside to teach literacy and present their political ideas. The education system in Russia lagged behind Europe and North American countries, keeping most peasants uneducated. As of 1877, about 78.9 percent of the Russian population was considered illiterate.

The populists' slogan, "To the People," came from Aleksandr Herzen, whose ideas led to populism. Herzen declared that Russia's future was its peasants. From London, where Herzen lived in exile, he wrote to his followers, "Go to the people. That is where you belong, exiles from science, soldiers of the Russian nation."[21] Another populist, Pyotr Lavrov, agreed: "Our social revolution will come from the country, not the towns."[23]

These well-intentioned reformers met with suspicion and resistance in rural areas. The peasants had been kept uninformed about many things and were often wary of outsiders. During the cholera epidemic of 1891–1892, peasants in towns along the Volga attacked hospitals and doctors who had come there to aid the sick. They accused these men of having poisoned their water, thus causing the epidemic. After several years, it seemed clear that the populist movement was failing to arouse the peasants.

Revolutionary Circles

Other kinds of revolutionary activities were going on during these same years. A group called Land and Liberty operated a secret printing press out of St. Petersburg. They circulated pamphlets and news sheets and also printed false identity papers and passports for people who needed them. Their spy network included a member who worked in the government's secret police.

While some groups wanted peaceful change, others used violence. Numerous acts of terrorism occurred between 1879 and 1881, often perpetrated by members of the People's Will. High-ranking officials were targeted for assassination; in fact, members of the group were responsible for assassinating Czar Alexander II. Most of the terrorists were eventually caught and sent to prison or executed.

Other people emerged to take their places. A group of young people planned to assassinate Alexander III in 1887. The plan was foiled by police and the conspirators were arrested and hanged. Among them was nineteen-year-old Aleksandr Ilyich Ulyanov. At his trial, Ulyanov told the judges, "There is no better way of dying than to lay down one's life for one's country. Such death does not fill honest and sincere men with any fear."[23] Among those who mourned for Aleksandr Ulyanov was his younger brother Vladimir, who would work for the Bolshevik cause under the new name of Lenin.

Many student revolutionaries turned to Marxism. Study circles of young intellectuals and students met to discuss these new ideas. Some of them began meeting with groups of the poor to teach them to read. They used library materials, books, globes, and maps while teaching classes throughout St. Petersburg and Moscow. Sometimes they handed out populist and Marxist literature.

Nineteen-year-old Aleksandr Ulyanov was hanged in 1887 for conspiring to assassinate Czar Alexander III.

Lenin Joins the Fight

A Marxist circle flourished in St. Petersburg. Lenin joined this circle in September 1893. He published pamphlets that described the hardships faced by workers, firmly believing that workers would join his cause once they saw the connection between their daily problems and the revolutionary agenda. Lenin hoped working-class Russians would realize that change was possible. He wrote,

> The Russian Social-Democratic Party declares its task to be helping the struggle of the Russian working class by developing labor's class consciousness, assisting its organization and showing it the real goals of the struggle.[24]

Alarmed by the rising number of people joining revolutionary groups, the government passed a law in 1894 that banned students from holding meetings or organizing clubs. In 1895, Lenin was arrested for his revolutionary speeches and writings and sent to exile in Siberia. He would spend two years there but continued to write and communicate with his followers, who met for the first official congress of the Social Democratic Workers' Party in March 1898. After leaving Siberia, Lenin lived in exile in western Europe, where he worked on his book *What Is to Be Done?*, published in 1902.

The Russian communist known as Lenin led the Bolshevik revolutionaries who called for rapid changes in Russian government.

A fellow revolutionary wrote of Lenin, "There is no other man who is absorbed by the revolution twenty-four hours a day, who has no other thoughts but the thought of revolution, and who, when he sleeps, dreams of nothing but the revolution."[25]

In 1899, there was another significant demonstration in Russia. University students in St. Petersburg protested the use of police force to disperse student gatherings. They paraded along the streets in school uniforms and organized a general strike that shut down schools all over Russia. The government responded by arresting numerous students, expelling hundreds, and drafting them into the Russian army.

Despite the threat of arrest, revolutionaries continued to meet and organize. The So-cial Democratic Workers' Party held a second congress in July and August of 1903. At that time, the group split into two factions, the Mensheviks and the Bolsheviks. The Mensheviks favored more gradual change and reform in the political system; the Bolsheviks wanted more rapid, thorough change. These two groups would play a prominent role throughout the revolutionary period.

A Disastrous War

Except for using police power to stifle revolutionary activity, the government did not address the people's concerns. In 1904, several of the czar's ministers suggested that he might unite the Russian people and encourage patriotism by conducting "a small, victorious war."[26]

As a target, they chose Japan. Russian troops were ordered into Korea, and when the Japanese arrived to drive them back, the Russo-Japanese War began. Russia suffered heavy casualties and was no match for the Japanese navy. When the war ended in August 1905, the government was harshly criticized for having involved the nation in such a fiasco. Before the year ended, Nicholas II would again greatly upset his people.

Bloody Sunday

To survey the activities of workers in St. Petersburg, police enlisted the help of a respected Orthodox priest, Father Gapon. Gapon came from a peasant family in Ukraine and had long believed in social reform as well as nonviolence. As he ministered to factory workers, he urged them to avoid alcohol and gambling. He organized the Union of Russian Factory Workers, a movement that spread across the country. The police saw in Gapon a desirable leader, someone they need not fear and might even encourage.

In January, metalworkers in St. Petersburg went on a strike that lasted four days. However, the strike had no impact on the government, so Gapon decided on something more dramatic. He wrote a letter to the czar, explaining to him that his ministers were not keeping him informed about the real state of affairs in Russia.

Lenin: The Path to Leadership

The most dedicated leader of the revolution, and future head of the new Russia, was Vladimir Ilyich Ulyanov. He was born in 1870 in Simbirsk, a small town on the Volga River, to a family of hereditary nobles that was not wealthy but quite comfortable. His father, a teacher of physics and mathematics, was Russian; his mother was German-Russian. Vladimir Ulyanov, who would later change his name to Lenin, was the third of seven children. They were religious, industrious people, and Vladimir was an outstanding student. When he graduated from high school, his headmaster wrote,

> Very gifted, always neat and assiduous, Ulyanov was first in all his subjects, and upon completing his studies received a gold medal as the most deserving pupil with regard to his ability, progress, and behavior. Neither in the school, nor outside, has a single instance been observed when he has given cause for dissatisfaction by word or deed. . . . I have had occasion to note a somewhat excessive tendency towards isolation and reserve.

The headmaster specifically noted the young man's good behavior since the family had recently experienced grief and scandal. The oldest brother, Aleksandr, was hanged in May 1887 for having joined in a plot to kill Czar Alexander III. The czar signed a warrant to have the five student conspirators executed. A year earlier, Vladimir's father had died, so his mother had gone alone to St. Petersburg to plead for mercy for her son, to no avail.

Remarkably, Vladimir finished the school year calmly and took his final exams. His mother tried to interest him in farming, but Vladimir was drawn to the same political ideas that had led to his brother's death. At the University of Kazan, where he majored in law, Lenin was expelled after only three months for taking part in a student protest meeting.

He went on to work in a law office in St. Petersburg, where he met his future wife, a schoolteacher named Nadezhda Krupskaya. Both were dedicated Marxists and joined the Social Democratic Party. They married in 1898 while in exile in Siberia for their revolutionary activities. Because he had money, Lenin did not suffer greatly in exile. He was able to maintain a home with servants, swim, fish, and pursue his reading and writing. When he was sent to Siberia late in 1896, he carried with him a trunk containing one hundred books.

The term in Siberia did not deter him from attacking the government. After he left, he was more vocal than ever. Using the pen name Lenin, he edited a revolutionary magazine called *Iskra* (the *Spark*), which was smuggled into Russia from abroad, and wrote fiery materials that made him famous among his peers. Often, his essays attacked the czar, whom the revolutionaries called "Nicholas the Bloody" and "Nicholas the Hangman."

Feminist Leader

Women played an active role in revolutionary groups and activities. One of the most prominent woman revolutionaries was Aleksandra Kollontay, a Bolshevik feminist born to an aristocratic family in 1872. Her maternal grandparents were a Finnish merchant and a Russian noblewoman; her paternal grandparents were both Ukrainian. Kollontay's father, a military officer, reached the rank of general. Her mother was unusually independent for a woman of her class and time.

Surrounded by vast poverty, this family enjoyed fine homes and clothing, servants, and opportunities for education and travel. They joined other socially concerned members of the educated nobility who pushed the Russian monarchy for reform.

In 1893, Aleksandra married engineer Vladimir Kollontay, a man of lesser means and social status with whom she had fallen in love. The couple had a son, Mikhail (Misha), in 1894. She continued her studies and wrote fiction, but felt stifled by marriage and motherhood. Kollontay told friends they kept her from her work.

Kollontay soon began writing about feminist issues. In those days, women lived with many legal and social restrictions. Among other things, a Russian woman could not obtain a passport without her husband's permission and could not own property. A man's testimony outweighed a woman's in a trial. Kollontay also criticized her family's noble lifestyle and her husband's lack of intellectual and political interests. The couple grew farther apart as she became more active in revolutionary activities. She gradually rejected her parents' liberalism in favor of socialism.

By 1905, Kollontay was well known as a Social Democrat and Menshevik and served as a courier for the movement, transporting letters, written materials, and money. She wrote that she and other young Russians "longed for a great mission in life. We reached out eagerly for a new belief."

In the years that followed, Kollontay continued to voice strong opinions, opposing Russian involvement in World War I. After the revolution, she offended some Communist Party leaders by opposing the strictness and inflexibility of the new regime. However, she remained a political force. Starting in 1922, Kollontay was posted to various countries, including Sweden, as an ambassador.

Bolshevik feminist Aleksandra Kollontay spoke out against legal and social restrictions in the lives of Russian women.

The people believe in Thee. They have made up their minds to gather at the Winter Palace tomorrow at 2 P.M. to lay their needs before Thee. . . . Do not fear anything. Stand tomorrow before the people and accept our humblest petition.[27]

It is not known whether Czar Nicholas received or read this letter. He had left the city with his family for Tsarskoe Selo and did not reply. At any rate, the czar did not show any desire to meet with workers or listen to their demands. He did not return to the palace in

St. Petersburg again, and lived at Tsarskoe Selo from that time on.

The thirty-two-year-old Gapon proceeded to organize the march to the Winter Palace to present a petition to the emperor. On January 22, men, women, and children gathered for the march. The crowd swelled to include an estimated two hundred thousand people. Gapon headed the five long lines of people, who bore religious icons and pictures of the czar. They trod through the snow, singing "God Save the Czar."

Their petition, carried by Father Gapon, asked the czar to institute an eight-hour workday with no overtime and a wage of at least one ruble per day (which equaled about fifty cents). They also asked for an assembly of representatives. Outside the Winter Palace, they waited hopefully for the czar to appear and personally receive their petition.

Fearing serious riots, the minister of the interior ordered military officers to stand outside the palace. These men ordered the crowd to leave, but the marchers ignored their commands, believing strongly in the justice of their cause and convinced that the czar was going to hear their requests.

Suddenly, shots rang out as the palace guard began firing at the crowd, mostly from distances of only ten to twenty yards. Chaos followed, with masses of people screaming and trying to flee from the gunfire. People cried out in fear and pain. Voices in the crowd could be heard shouting, "The Czar will not help us!"[28]

When the shooting stopped, the snow-lined square around the palace was stained with blood. More than five hundred people were dead, and thousands more had been wounded.

This infamous day became known as Bloody Sunday. Father Gapon managed to escape arrest by fleeing to Finland. He was enraged by the carnage in St. Petersburg. He wrote a widely published letter to Czar Nicholas with these ominous words:

The innocent blood of workers, their wives and children, lies forever between thee, oh

On what came to be known as Bloody Sunday, military officers barricaded the Winter Palace of Nicholas II. When a crowd of two hundred thousand Russian citizens approached, the defenders opened fire.

soul destroyer, and the Russian people. . . . Let all the blood that has to be shed, hangman, fall upon thee and thy kindred![29]

Bloody Sunday marked a turning point in the way average Russians viewed their czar. Now many saw Nicholas as a heartless man who cared nothing about his humbler subjects. Some called him a murderer.

Life in St. Petersburg grew more violent and unpredictable as strikes and demonstrations increased. Among these strikes was the May 1905 "comma strike," which took place in Moscow. Printers who did piecework went

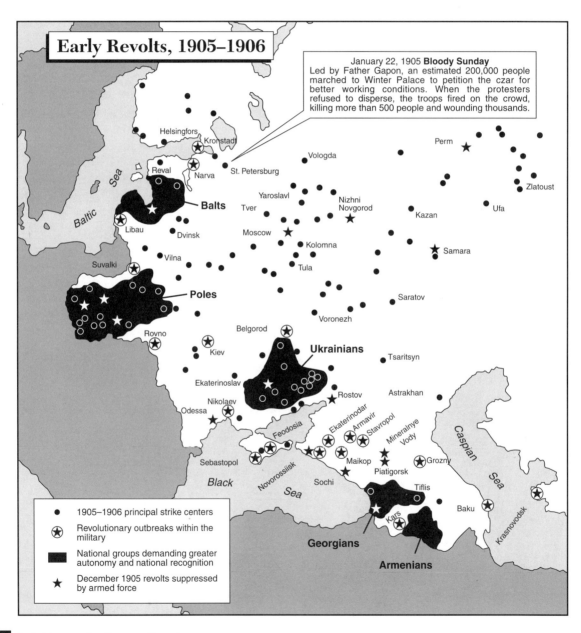

Early Revolts, 1905–1906

January 22, 1905 **Bloody Sunday**
Led by Father Gapon, an estimated 200,000 people marched to Winter Palace to petition the czar for better working conditions. When the protesters refused to disperse, the troops fired on the crowd, killing more than 500 people and wounding thousands.

- ● 1905–1906 principal strike centers
- ⊛ Revolutionary outbreaks within the military
- ■ National groups demanding greater autonomy and national recognition
- ★ December 1905 revolts suppressed by armed force

on strike to demand higher wages. Railroad workers and others joined them. The people of Moscow had no newspapers, streetcar service, or postal services. Bakeries, law offices, banks, and telegraph offices shut down. Red banners and posters urging revolution cropped up more and more in the streets.

After Bloody Sunday, men in the military also showed their anger toward the imperial government. There was rising discontent, especially among Russian soldiers who had been forced to fight in the Russo-Japanese War. These men had been sent out ill equipped and unprepared. Their navy lacked strong ships and armaments. Many had not been trained to properly identify and then overtake Japanese warships, so casualties increased. These men, who no longer felt the same loyalty toward their czar, would later be willing to fight against the empire that had let them down.

Terrorism also surged in this atmosphere. The number of terrorist plots increased dramatically after Bloody Sunday. Government officials had good reason to fear for their lives. During 1905, more than fifteen hundred officials were assassinated.

Revolutionaries living in exile were encouraged by news of this disorder. Lenin wrote letters to Russia urging more terrorism and told his followers to use, among other things, "rifles, revolvers, bombs, brass knuckles, clubs, [and] rags soaked in oil to start fires with."[30]

The Czar Answers

People pressing for reform led Czar Nicholas II to reluctantly issue the October Manifesto, a few reforms that led to an end of the large strike. Some of the czar's ministers also urged him to make concessions instead of quelling the disorder with police power. Nicholas gave up some of his power to the legislature, the Duma, in a new constitution, the first constitution Russia had ever had. This was significant, since the czar was departing from total autocracy. However, the constitution let the czar maintain all control over the army and navy and handle all matters related to foreign policy and the Ministry of the Interior.

The Duma (from a Russian word meaning "advice") was to have members elected by the people. They and the Imperial Council, half of whose members were chosen by the czar, would share the authority of advising the czar, but he was free to issue imperial decrees when the Duma was not in session. Nicholas felt ambivalent about the Duma.

Many Russians were still not satisfied. Sailors on the battleship *Potemkin* in the Black Sea staged an angry mutiny. The leader of the mutiny was arrested and executed. Other revolts in various military installations were also stopped by the czar's police. On December 9, police arrested the leader of the Soviet committee in St. Petersburg. Menshevik Leon Trotsky took over his position and organized the workers to refuse to pay taxes. Trotsky was arrested for these activities, but Lenin and other leaders had returned to Russia to move things along.

Revolutionary activities had been widespread in 1905. Although people throughout Russia were not united against the government, more were talking about the future. Many had given their lives to the cause. By year's end, almost 15,000 were dead, more than 18,000 wounded, and 79,000 imprisoned. The country was aroused.

5 Power Struggles

Although Russia now had a constitution and a legislature, the czar did not want to relinquish much power. He struggled to maintain his regime while his political opponents pressed for change. More militant forces continued their struggle in the factories, streets, universities, and underground press.

When the first Duma met in May 1906 at the Tauride Palace in St. Petersburg, it was a rather conservative group committed to slow, steady change. Among it were 150 members of the Kadets (Constitutional Democratic) Party, mostly members of the gentry and middle class. Another 100 men, the Social Revolutionaries, represented the working class and peasants.

The members of the Duma presented the czar with a list of limited reforms they hoped he would make. Land reform was a prime concern. The Duma wanted the czar to distribute some estate lands to the peasants and to reduce burdensome taxes. It also wanted a sharp reduction in the power of the secret police. The czar upset members of the Duma by not appearing in person to answer their requests. Instead, he sent a representative, who informed them the reforms were unacceptable.

An angry Duma voted to censure the imperial government, an unprecedented step in czarist Russia. For two months, Duma members criticized the government's position. The czar finally responded by dissolving the Duma, and locking members out of the Tauride Palace when they arrived on July 22 for another session.

This struggle for power continued for more than a decade, rousing indignation against the czar and his advisers. With each new decision, the imperial family became increasingly unpopular.

In this atmosphere, revolutionary leaders gained more support, especially among intellectuals. Trade unions grew and more members of all classes began to favor a revolution that would completely change the government. Other people wanted reforms that would greatly reduce the czar's power and turn Russia into a constitutional monarchy. Still others thought Russia should be a czarless democracy. Leaders of different parties were even willing to unite because they believed it would promote a revolution. However, revolutionaries were constantly on guard, watched by police and informers. They were often arrested, exiled, or imprisoned.

A Dynamic Leader

The czar managed to calm people somewhat in 1906 by resurrecting the Duma and installing Pyotr Stolypin as its new prime minister. A native of provincial Russia, Stolypin impressed people with his straightforward speaking style and efficiency. When a new Duma was elected, the prime minister urged land reform. Members of the Duma called Stolypin a gifted leader. The czar wrote to his mother, "I have come to like and respect this man."[31]

However, Czarina Alexandra opposed Stolypin and worked to get him dismissed. She resented his power and later said, "Never mention that man to me. He was overshadowing his Emperor."[32]

Stolypin worked with the Duma and the czar to achieve key reforms. As a result of his efforts, a new class of peasant landowners developed, because peasants could own and buy land for the first time. (By 1916, 6.5 million peasant families would live on their own land, accounting for three-quarters of the farmland in Russia.)

While many praised these reforms, zealous revolutionaries were wary. Lenin, for example, worried that the movement might die if people became satisfied with the progress that was occurring. He wrote pessimistically, "I do not expect to see the revolution."[33] Stolypin's success also angered wealthy conservative Russians, who did not want to lose their land or wealth. Some members of the Duma resented his efforts to limit their power, but Stolypin said this was necessary to prevent the czar from disbanding the Duma again.

On September 1, 1911, Stolypin's enemies took violent action. He was assassinated while sitting during intermission at the royal opera in Kiev. Czar Nicholas and his two oldest daughters had been sitting near Stolypin but left their seats during the intermission. Nicholas described an account of the murder to his mother:

> Women were shrieking and, directly in front of me in the stalls, Stolypin was standing; he slowly turned his face towards us and with his left hand made the sign of the cross in the air. Only then did I notice that he was very pale and that his right hand and uniform were bloodstained. He slowly sank into his chair.[34]

People in the crowd tried to lynch Stolypin's killer, but the police took him into custody. The czar and his daughters left at eleven o'clock after this wrenching evening. Stolypin's assassin was hanged on September 9.

Appointed prime minister in 1906, Pyotr Stolypin helped usher in key reforms for the Russian people, especially the peasant class. He was assassinated by political enemies in 1911.

An Unstable Society

The czar replaced Stolypin with a more conservative man. With Stolypin gone, revolutionaries became more active again. The number of striking workers soared in 1912. When gold miners in Lena stopped working in April, the local police fired on them, arousing the people's anger. In 1909, some eight thousand workers had taken part in strikes; in 1912, that number soared to five hundred thousand. Within two years, more than a million Russians would publicly demonstrate to express their political frustrations.

As time went on, members of the Duma became increasingly bold and were willing to attack imperial policies. Some took on more active roles. Duma member Aleksandr Kerensky visited Lena after police crushed the miners' strike. Shocked by stories about police brutality, he returned more determined than ever to enact reforms.

Hypnotic "Healer": Rasputin

The Duma also launched an official investigation of one of the most infamous figures of this era: Grigory Yefimovich Rasputin. Rasputin was born to a peasant family in Siberia in 1872. Although he was not an educated person and had not been ordained by the church, he wore priest's garb, including a long, black cassock. Rasputin wandered from town to town, presenting himself as a spiritual leader and healer. People offered him food and lodging and sought his help and guidance.

After he arrived in St. Petersburg in 1905, Rasputin charmed his way into high society. With his long, thick hair and beard, he had an imposing appearance. One admirer commented on his "most extraordinary eyes, large, light, brilliant." Another observer, who called his gaze "cunning," said that Rasputin "carried with him a strong animal smell, like the smell of a goat."[35]

A noblewoman in St. Petersburg became so taken with Rasputin that she invited him to live at her mansion and introduced him to her friends. While some people criticized the "monk's" crude table manners, sexual escapades, drunkenness, and frequently dirty appearance, his supporters ignored or disbelieved these things. Instead, they revered his so-called spiritual powers.

The royal couple had sought out mystics, clairvoyants, seers, and holy men of various

Though investigated as a fraud and criticized for his coarse behavior, Grigory Rasputin, a self-proclaimed spiritual healer, was embraced by Empress Alexandra, who believed he could help heal her son.

types before. Now Alexandra was convinced that Rasputin was sent by God to help her incurably ill son; she was certain he had healing powers. Somehow Rasputin was able to ease Alexis's symptoms. His voice, words, and gaze seemed to reduce the boy's pain and help him sleep or even stop bleeding.

The empress became fanatically devoted to the man she called "our friend." In her letters, she described the peace and relief he brought with his visits, and in a 1909 letter, she called Rasputin "my beloved unforgettable teacher, redeemer, and mentor."[36]

As Rasputin's influence grew, some people bribed him to sway the czar. But Rasputin also attracted enemies. Spies followed him and made detailed reports about his drinking, womanizing, and disorderly conduct at taverns, parties, and private homes. Newspapers printed sensational stories and accusations against Rasputin, but the empress refused to listen. Before his assassination, Prime Minister Stolypin had ordered Rasputin out of St. Petersburg, and he returned for a time to his Siberian village.

Alexandra was deeply upset, especially when Czarevitch Alexis suffered a terrible attack during a family holiday in Poland. He fell out of a boat and was badly bruised, causing internal bleeding into his groin and thigh. The boy seemed close to death, lapsing in and out of consciousness. Rasputin received frantic telegrams from the empress. He sent back a message saying, "God has seen your tears and heard your prayers. Do not grieve. The Little One will not die."[37]

Alexandra told her husband to shut down the Duma again, or at least to expel Rasputin's harshest critics. She publicly snubbed the prime minister, Count Vladimir Kokovtsov, for she resented his decision to continue the investigation of Rasputin. In February 1914, Kokovtsov was dismissed. Rasputin returned to St. Petersburg, where he again became a powerful political force.

To avoid hurting his wife, Nicholas ignored those who warned him to spurn Rasputin. One day, the royal tutor saw the czar opening his mail. As he tossed a letter into the wastebasket, the czar said, "Another of those denunciations of Gregory. I get them almost every day and throw them away unread."[38] A British diplomat who knew Nicholas II later wrote, "It was his . . .

"They Think I Am Rather Abnormal"

As it became clearer that Empress Alexandra was making political decisions and choosing ministers, animosity toward the czar's wife intensified. Many Russians mistrusted their German-born czarina. The czar's enemies accused the couple of German sympathies, even treason.

The dowager empress Marie, mother of Czar Nicholas, feared Alexandra might destroy the monarchy. Late in 1916, she told her son he must get rid of his wife somehow—perhaps send her to a convent or mental institution. Once, she said, "My poor daughter-in-law does not perceive that she is ruining both the dynasty and herself. She sincerely believes in the holiness of an adventurer and we are powerless to ward off the misfortune which is sure to come."

The empress viewed herself as an intensely spiritual person misunderstood by others. She once said, "They think I am rather abnormal, but they are wrong. It is just that I am closer to heaven than I am to earth."

Empress Alexandra was not always in favor with the Russian people. Many distrusted her German ancestry and her influence in government affairs.

crowning tragedy to be Emperor and autocrat in such times and to be surrounded by sinister and fatal influences which he was probably too kindly-eyed to see, certainly too weak-willed to control."[39]

At War

While Russia endured inner turmoil and uncertain leadership, the world outside became embroiled in conflicts over territory. In August 1914, Russia joined its Western ally France to fight against Germany. Most of the Mensheviks and nearly all the Bolsheviks opposed Russian involvement. However, there was a surge of patriotic feeling when war was first declared. Ten thousand people cheered, "Lead us to victory!" and sang the national anthem when Nicholas and Alexandra appeared on the balcony of the Winter Palace in St. Petersburg, now called Petrograd.

The war became increasingly unpopular as food shortages and inflation spread, and millions of men, mostly peasants, were drafted. Wounded soldiers wrote to their families about the inadequate food and medical services. People grieved for dead family members. By 1916, between 6 and 8 million Russian soldiers had been killed, wounded, or imprisoned.

Many workers were also drafted, and those who remained became more politicized. Between 1914 and 1917, wages rose by about 100 percent, but at the same time, prices increased by 400 percent. The number of striking workers rose steadily to more than 1 million in 1916. The government used police force to firmly subdue strikes and other revolutionary activity. Government officials demanded faster production in factories making shells and other war materials.

The government could not stem the economic and administrative problems brought on by war. The czar made no major policy changes. His wife urged an iron hand. In letters to her husband, Alexandra wrote,

Be more autocratic, my very own sweetheart. . . . Russia, thank God, is not a constitutional country. . . . Be the Emperor, be Peter the Great, John the Terrible,

Rasputin, seated on the left, with ladies of Alexandra's court. Rasputin gained so much power through the empress that he eventually directed military strategy and was consulted for other affairs of state.

The populist movement of the 1800s failed to turn many peasants into revolutionaries, but during the 1900s they were much more politically aware. Ruth Bonner was born in Siberia in 1900, the descendant of individuals who were sent to Siberia as forced laborers. Interviewed by Richard Lourie, she recalled the lively political discussions that took place among family members in the years before the revolution:

> Once a year my grandfather's clan got together to sit down at the table for dinner and long discussions. About the revolution, persecution, prison, exile, whatever. The older children had theoretical arguments. The Socialist Revolutionaries argued with the Bolsheviks and the Mensheviks argued with the Socialist Revolutionaries and the anarchists. There were as many party positions at the table as there were children, each one trying to win the day. They discussed land reform, the working class, the situation of the working class, the need to increase the number of workers, the influx of workers from the country to the city. They all argued ferociously and sometimes fist fights broke out. Then my grandfather would step in.

Bonner's mother's family was more educated and had studied abroad. Of them, she said, "Those relatives were more conservative, more educated, more interested in art, literature, poetry and science. And they were somewhat removed from social problems and politics. Liberal democrats."

People found ways to rebel against the czarist system. During the prerevolutionary years, some peasants who disliked the government gave their children nontraditional names. For centuries, Russians had chosen the names of saints and people honored by the Russian Orthodox Church. Revolutionaries scorned traditional names like Igor and Ivan and used other names, sometimes made-up ones, such as Roi, which means "to dig."

Emperor Paul—crush them all under you. . . . We have been placed by God on the throne, and we must keep it firm and give it over to our son untouched.[40]

At her urging, during 1915, twenty-one government ministers were dismissed, and men chosen by Rasputin replaced them.

During the war, Alexandra devoted herself to Red Cross work at military hospitals. She and her oldest daughters, Olga and Tatiana, qualified as Sisters of Mercy and could be seen wearing their nursing habits most of the time.

Nicholas continued to change his cabinet. Within three years, he appointed four different prime ministers, three ministers of foreign affairs, three different ministers of war, and five new ministers of the interior. The sixth minister of the interior, Aleksandr Protopopov, was a friend of Rasputin's, and many people thought him mentally unsound.

Rasputin's influence now expanded into more affairs of state. The czar's advisers were chosen or dismissed at Rasputin's will. During 1915 and 1916, the czar ordered his ministers to discuss all military plans with Rasputin, who had the power to approve or disapprove their plans.

Rasputin also decided military strategy, based on the divine insights attributed to him by Alexandra. She sent Rasputin's instructions to the czar, who often stayed at a military base. In September 1915, she wrote, "Don't forget, before the cabinet meeting, to hold up our friend's small icon and comb yourself several times with his comb." In 1916, she wrote, "Our friend asks you not to order an advance on the northern front."[41]

Friends warned the czar that people resented Rasputin and were turning against him. The Duma thought the czar was incompetent, but it lacked the power to override his decisions. Grand Duke Alexander warned his cousin Nicholas that the situation was dire, writing, "Strange as it may appear, it is the government itself which is busily paving the way for revolution."[42]

"Our Day Will Come"

By the end of 1916, anger and misery were felt throughout Russia. Farm produce could not be sold abroad, and many peasants refused to sell it to the government for worthless paper currency. The railway system no longer functioned, and candles, salt, and kerosene did not reach rural areas. People in the cities went hungry and complained of their working conditions. More than 15 million Russian men were serving in the military.

Police in Petrograd saw signs of unrest and anticipated an uprising. An official police report warned of "a threatening crisis that was about to explode. . . . We are on the eve of great events compared with which those of 1905 were mere child's play."[43]

In December 1916, the body of Rasputin was found floating in the Neva River. He had been poisoned, stabbed, beaten, and shot. Because the three killers were aristocrats and

close to the czar's family, they were not executed. Instead they were merely banished from Petrograd: Prince Felix Yusupov went to his country estate; Vladimir Purishkevich, a member of the Duma, was ordered to the army; Grand Duke Dmitri went to live in Persia.

The empress grieved quietly, as if in a trance, and she often prayed beside Rasputin's tomb. The czar isolated himself even from his close ministers, remaining with his family at Tsarskoe Selo.

Many Russians rejoiced that Rasputin was dead. They called the murderers heroes and lit candles in their honor at churches. People hoped the czar would now respond to their needs, but little changed. Many began considering drastic actions, including plots to

Interior minister Aleksandr Protopopov (right) was a friend of Rasputin. In attempts to curb popular unrest, Protopopov's policies actually prompted more rioting, leading many to think the minister unfit for his position.

Angry Soldiers

Despite initial feelings of patriotism, Russian soldiers fighting in World War I became disillusioned. They lacked ammunition, boots, clothing, and horseshoes. The food was poor, and supplies of grain, cereals, meat, and beans were inadequate. Weapons were so scarce that trainees shared the same rifle, and soldiers at the front hastened to retrieve the guns of comrades who died in action. The troops had no air support. Supplies and food failed to reach the troops because of inadequate transportation. Since army medics were often unavailable, wounded men had to wait for treatment.

By 1917, the amount of necessary supplies fell below 50 percent or more. About half of all able-bodied peasant men had been drafted, which meant fewer people were raising food. As a result, mass desertions took place, and ex-soldiers formed angry bands that attacked estates and took food.

The class system prevailed in military life as well as among civilians. Officers came from the higher classes and regarded the soldiers beneath them as social inferiors. Soldiers were required to address their superior officers as "Your Honor" or "Your Excellency," even when they were off duty. Laws banned them from using tramway carriages or from dining in restaurants.

Under these conditions, morale sagged. Officers lost faith in the ability of the czar and his advisers to wage a successful war.

General Yanushkevich said, "No amount of science can tell us how to wage war without ammunition, without rifles, and without guns."

kill the czar or to kidnap the family and prevent the czar from ruling. These plots were planned not just by radicals and revolutionaries but by members of the aristocracy, the military, and the Duma.

Advisers urged the czar to set up a popular government to avoid a crisis. He listened, instead, to his powerful minister of the interior, who was ignored in the Duma. Protopopov, was a friend of the royal couple and misled them about how the people regarded their czar. Out of touch with the real mood in Russia, in December 1916, Alexandra wrote to her husband that "a great and magnificent epoch is dawning for your reign."[44]

Revolutionaries saw a different picture. They communicated their frustrations to Lenin, who was living in exile in Switzerland. On February 19, 1917, Lenin wrote to his close friend Inessa Armand, describing letters he had received from Russia: "They write that the mood of the masses is a good one, that chauvinism [strong feelings of patriotism] is clearly declining, and that probably our day will come."[45]

Peace! Land! Bread!

The year 1917 began with tension and uncertainty. There were bitter labor strikes, and people demonstrated in the streets calling for food and lower prices. On the war front, ill-equipped soldiers became increasingly resentful and unwilling to fight for the imperial government. In January, a professor in Petrograd wrote,

> University life tends to become more and more disorderly. On the walls of lavatories one reads such sentences as: "Down With the Czar!" "Death to the Czarina of Rasputin!" "Long Life to the Revolution!" These have been erased by the police, but immediately they reappear. The newspapers have become audacious in attacking the Government. . . . Today I met three soldiers, friends of mine, just returned from the front. One of them spoke with such hatred against the Government, the expressions of the others of indignation and discontent in the army were so extreme that they shocked me. The army then may precipitate the Revolution.[46]

The professor, Pitirim Sorokin, described a population that looked more and more rebellious. Women and children demonstrated in the streets calling for bread and herring. Large, noisy riots stopped the flow of tramcars, as people plundered shops and even attacked policemen. As February drew near, he wrote,

> The orderly routine of life is broken. Shops and offices are closed. In the University, instead of lectures, political meetings are held. Newspapers appear irregularly. Revolution has pushed one foot over the threshold of my country. . . . Crowds on the Nevsky Prospekt are larger. The police are idle and irresolute. One hears that even the Cossacks have refused to disperse the crowds. This means that the Government is helpless and their machine broken. Rioters have begun to kill policemen.[47]

Diamonds and Champagne

The aristocracy went on with their lives, seemingly oblivious to the mood of the people. Theaters and the ballet had large audiences, and the best city restaurants did brisk business. A Frenchman who visited Petrograd in February wrote in surprise,

> Never before have I seen so many cars in the streets, so many diamonds glittering on the shoulders of women. All the theatres were crammed. The fashionable restaurants were the scene of incessant orgies; a bottle of champagne fetched a hundred roubles [which amounted to five times more than most workers earned in a month] and people amused themselves by pouring it out by the bucket.[48]

The Russian aristocracy continued to live lavishly despite war rations and rioting in the streets.

In February 1917, the royal couple hosted a rare party at the Alexander Palace in Tsarskoe Selo to honor several British diplomats. Servants lit the porcelain stoves and crystal chandeliers. Bouquets of lilies, mimosa, lilacs, irises, and hyacinths graced the public rooms. Empress Alexandra wore a cream silk gown with silver and blue embroidery, her trademark diamonds adorning her wrists and red-gold hair. Guests sat at the grand table in the long crimson and silver dining room.

Because of war rationing, the royal family had been eating plain dinners, with little sugar or butter. Meat was served no more than twice per week. That night, to honor their guests, they dined far more lavishly, on cream of barley soup, trout, roast veal, chicken and cucumber salad, and tangerine ice.

It was the last state dinner the Romanovs would ever give.

On the Brink

Revolutionary fervor gripped the capital in February. In the Duma, the more liberal and radical members pushed for a new government. Though Social Democrats and others disagreed with them on some points, they shared their contempt for the powerful interior minister, Protopopov. Aleksandr Kerensky, an emerging Socialist leader, made numerous antiwar speeches.

In February, more men and women took to marching in the streets. As the number of workers who joined them increased, factories had to close down. Thousands of leaflets were handed out, urging workers to rise up against the regime. Bread rationing was enforced as of March 1. People rushed to the bakeries, and women staged large demonstrations. Metalworkers went on strike. The various political parties were still not united and had not organized or planned these demonstrations.

Duma president Michael Rodzianko wrote to warn the czar of impending doom. He received no reply. Nicholas was preparing to return to army headquarters, where he would arrive the second week of March. From Mogilev, he wrote to his wife that he looked forward to some leisure time, saying, "I shall take up dominoes again."[49]

Rising up against the monarchy, the Russian people left their jobs in factories and protested in the streets of Petrograd in 1917.

"Give Us Bread"

The Russian people, on the other hand, wanted food. A large women's strike had been planned in Petrograd for a long time, set for March 8, traditionally International Women's Day. The night before the strike, women met in the Lesony textile factory, where they adopted their slogans, "Down with the autocracy" and "Down with the war."

The following day, these hundreds of women were joined by about one hundred thousand workers who gathered in the streets. As they marched, people chanted, "Give us bread." A number of bakeries were looted that day and the next, as more strikers and women joined the demonstration. Some used sticks, cobblestones, or chunks of ice as weapons, but police did not fire into the crowds. The government refrained from sending out soldiers or Cossacks to disperse them.

As the demonstration went on, there was some shooting in the streets, and traffic halted for hours at a time. Nonetheless, most people went about their business. Alan Moorehead writes,

> The everyday things of life went on and got mixed up in the oddest way with the fighting. A milkman's van was seen trundling down the Nevsky Prospekt at the moment when the police were getting ready to fire; and when the firing did start groups of women typists could be seen looking down from the upper windows as though some kind of parade was going on, a ceremony for some visiting celebrity.[50]

The British ambassador, Sir George Buchanan, wrote to his superiors in London on March 9: "Some disorders occurred here today but nothing serious."[51]

The mobs in the street were spontaneous for the most part. The crowd seemed to gain strength as more people took their anger into the streets. Seizing the opportunity, leaders of various political parties formed a strike committee to organize and widen the strike. The crowds grew larger and noisier. Some were bold enough to attack places and people associated with the czarist government, including the Winter Palace, courts, the jails, St. Paul's Cathedral, and the military arsenal. According to Pitirim Sorokin, "From where we stood we could see the red glow of a fire near the Nicolaevsky Station." The police station was on fire. Someone in the mob told him, "We are going to destroy all Government offices, burn, smash, kill all police, all tyrants, all despots!"[52]

Revolution!

Between March 8 and March 10, the demonstrations grew larger. On March 9, Czar Nicholas ordered a halt to the demonstrations. The next day, a Saturday, it was estimated that the size of the crowds swelled to three hundred thousand. The government banned all public meetings and assemblies.

But the people refused to disperse. On March 11, they marched defiantly with red banners, crying, "Down with Protopopov!" and "Down with the German woman" (Czarina Alexandra). Mobs attacked and looted police stations, jails, and court buildings. Fires were set throughout Petrograd, and the mayor was shot.

On International Women's Day, March 8, 1918, hundreds of Russian women joined in the political demonstrations in Petrograd, marching and chanting, "Give us bread."

The Bolsheviks and other groups who wished to bring down the czar helped the demonstrators. Underground groups furnished money, hiding places, and leadership to the people now agitating against the government.

Several important factors worked in their favor. The police in Petrograd, who numbered more than 160,000 armed men, were no longer the career policemen who worked there prior to the war. These replacements were younger and less loyal and included men from Estonia and other countries that bordered Russia, places that had suffered greatly during the war years. Other replacements were elderly men who had been reservists. The Cossacks were not geared to fight in city streets. Besides, many of these men sympathized with the workers and others who were demonstrating.

Soldiers were sent out, but they, too, declined to take strong action. When a company of the Volinsk Regiment was ordered to fire, they aimed their rifles toward the sky, not the crowds. Another unit rebelled and killed their commander. Later, however, some soldiers did fire at the crowds in Znamenskaya Square. About sixty people were killed, and others were wounded.

The Revolt Spreads

Army units soon joined the revolutionaries. On March 12, members of the Volinsk and

A mob burns the royal coat of arms. Such brazen acts of disloyalty often went unpunished because the military and the police forces refused to deal harshly with the protesters.

Ready to Revolt

Ivan Vrachov was born in 1897 in the Kuban Cossack region of Russia. He later recalled the lack of opportunities open to a poor child in czarist Russia:

> My father was a stoker [of furnaces], my mother a cook and a washerwoman. I had three years of the local parochial school. . . . My parents tried to enroll me in the city elementary school, which had first through eighth, but I wasn't accepted. I wasn't accepted because I was from a poor family. And when one of my teachers tried to get me assigned to the high school—I was a good student—there turned out to be an insurmountable obstacle. The Tsar's minister of education had decreed, it was right there in black and white, that the children of cooks were not to be admitted to high schools.

Vrachov had to go to work at age eleven. He worked in a brewery, then in a noodle factory. Later, he learned to cut hair and apply makeup, which enabled him to work in a theater.

An inspiring teacher instilled a love of reading in Vrachov, and he read Russian classics and the progressive magazine *Chronicle* by Gorky, as well as literature from revolutionary groups. Vrachov became involved in the antiwar movement in 1915 as his feelings of patriotism dwindled. He was, as he says, "100 percent prepared" when the revolution began in 1917.

> There were hundreds like me from the working class who took an active hand in the revolution. And some of us ended up in the highest echelons of the [Communist] party. The revolution flung open doors for people with energy and questioning minds, minds that were of course taken by revolution's ideas.

other regiments came out against their czar. The government no longer had the use of the army. As the Cossacks observed these mutinies, they relinquished their neutrality in support of the revolution. At Tsarskoe Selo, the empress's garrison mutinied, and she could not be moved to a safer location. She would not have left anyway, because all her children had measles, and the czarina insisted on caring for them where they were.

Only about two thousand loyal troops remained—too few to control the huge crowds in Petrograd, which were looting and seizing arms from arsenals. Revolutionary groups forced army officers out of the Astoria Hotel. They set fire to the District Court. The mobs proceeded to the Tauride Palace, singing "La Marseillaise," the anthem of the French Revolution. Fearing for their lives, some members of the Duma went into hiding.

The czar ordered his military commander in Petrograd, General Sergey Khabalov, to end the disorder, and the czar issued an edict disbanding the Duma. On March 12, Nicholas finally agreed to return to Petrograd and discuss forming a new government with his advisers and the leaders of the Duma. It was too late. Railway workers identified the czar's train and blocked the line. Nicholas had to head in another direction.

Duma leaders inside the Tauride Palace realized the regime could not regain control.

Kerensky wanted to support the revolutionaries, but others hesitated. Political parties formed emergency committees to make plans for a new government and handle military affairs and the distribution of wages and food. Bolsheviks formed the Ex Com; others formed the Duma Committee, which opposed some Bolshevik positions. The Duma Committee was officially in charge, and it controlled the treasury. Yet the Ex Com put armed Red Guards in the streets and used its veto power in the Duma.

On March 13 came the final collapse. Troops that had supported the czar switched to the rebels' side. The government announced these casualties: 1,315 dead or wounded, including 53 officers, 602 soldiers, 73 policemen, and 587 civilians. A large red banner now flew from the Winter Palace.

End of the Dynasty

It was from inside his railroad car, heading toward military headquarters in Pskov, that Nicholas II ended his reign as czar. Before abdicating the throne, the czar sent for the court physician, who confirmed that Alexis could never be cured. The czar then abdicated in favor of his brother Grand Duke Michael. The grand duke declined the title the next day, and czarism ended in Russia.

Margarita Ivanovna Zarudny, age nine in 1917, lived in a village in the countryside. She recalls that people seemed happy and optimistic after the czar abdicated.

A platform covered with red cloth was built in the village square. People went to the platform and spoke, congratulating everyone on their new freedoms. The Tsar had abdicated. He had not been killed and was in no danger. There was going to be a democratic government. Everybody was very happy."[53]

Nicholas Romanov, now an ordinary citizen, planned to take his family to England by ship. However, the Romanovs were forbidden to leave and were instead placed under guard at their home. Under pressure from some Socialists in the Duma, the provisional government agreed that the czar and his family should be kept in Russia under arrest to prevent any counterrevolutionary plots.

Provisional Government

With the czar no longer in charge, what form would a new government take? Some members of the Duma set out to shape that new government, but moderate members found themselves in conflict with the Bolsheviks.

A revolutionary student group had arrested Protopopov and other strongly czarist ministers. They were locked inside a room in the palace with other political prisoners. Some were relieved to be in custody, because they feared the mobs outside might kill them. Inside the palace, numerous soldiers moved about, guarding one group or another. The Ex Com occupied one wing, while the Duma Committee used another. Workers and various factory leaders, bankers, and others met with Ex Com and Duma Committee members to advise them.

Some Bolsheviks, Mensheviks, and members of other leftist groups formed the Petrograd Soviet under leader Nikolay Chkheidze. As more people arrived, a larger room had to be found to hold the more than two thousand participants. Soldiers' delegates at the meeting said, "We refuse to serve against the people anymore, we're going to join with our brother workers."[54]

As the Duma members formed a provisional government, it seemed that the revolution was over. The city had suffered little damage, and there were few casualties considering the number of people involved. The 184 who died were placed in red coffins, and a million people marched quietly past their graves in Petrograd. At first, the provisional government declared that no religious services would be held, but the victims' families expressed misgivings, so priests went to bless the graves.

People in other towns and cities had followed the lead of the workers in Petrograd. Telegrams brought news of their successful fight. Authorities in Moscow and outlying villages decided to accept the authority of the new provisional government and its committees. The chief of police in Moscow told a crowd of people, "Long live the Revolution!"[55] Red flags were hung on buildings throughout the city, as in Petrograd. People tied red ribbons on their hats and coats to show they supported the revolution.

At the end of March, Lenin was still in Switzerland, seeking to obtain the papers and transportation he and his wife needed to return to Russia. He expressed his impatience: "You can imagine what a torture it is for us to be stuck here at a time like this."[56] The forty-seven-year-old revolutionary finally reached Russia by train in the spring and was greeted by thousands of supporters. At once, he began to denounce the provisional government.

Unmet Needs

The new government, led by Socialist Aleksandr Kerensky, faced many problems, and the three main demands of the people—peace, land, and bread—had not been satisfied.

With so many different political parties, it was difficult to reach a consensus about how to govern Russia. Liberals, moderates, and conservatives wanted to restore order and

"Take Care of This Heritage"

During the revolution, mobs and individuals looted and destroyed property, especially statues, portraits, and other images of the czar. Concerned leaders and citizens tried to prevent massive damage to property or land. When the Bolshevik Party met for its April conference in 1917, they adopted Lenin's resolution regarding the land: "The Party advises peasants to seize the land in an organized manner, not to damage property, and to increase agricultural production."

The revolutionaries would also heed socialist author Maksim Gorky, who urged them not to harm or destroy places of cultural and historic importance:

Citizens, the old masters have gone away and a great heritage is left behind. Now it belongs to the whole people. Citizens, take care of this heritage, take care of the palaces—they will become palaces of your national art; take care of the pictures, the statues, the buildings—they are the embodiment of the spiritual power of yourselves and of your forefathers. Art is the beauty which talented people were able to create even under despotic oppression and which bears witness to the power and beauty of the human soul.

continue the war alongside the Allies. The Ex Com, made up of Mensheviks, Bolsheviks, and Social Revolutionaires, hoped to end Russia's involvement in World War I and move toward socialism, a system in which the means of production, whether it be a factory, farm, or mine, are commonly owned by a social group, instead of by private owners. Most people wanted to end the war. Moscow and other cities formed soviets—elected committees—that attempted to keep order and meet social needs. These committees passed decrees and organized police units. They also rationed food and opened distribution centers.

Life in Russia was chaotic as a new form of government took shape. Politicians wrote fiery articles in newspapers, and made speeches on the streets or in meeting halls.

Because most people were still illiterate, they were more easily influenced by powerful speakers. Loud protesters, sometimes as many as five hundred thousand a day in Petrograd, lined the streets until after dark. Most of them were workers and soldiers, but there were many women and peasants, too. One day in May, soldiers who had been disabled or wounded in the war marched in support of the provisional government. Another day, some soldiers demanded to be allowed to return to the country for the harvest, carrying signs that read, "Our families are dying of hunger."

Wealthy Russians often found their homes taken over by revolutionaries. Among the finest homes in Petrograd was that of Mathilde Kschessinskaya, premier dancer for

In Petrograd crowds celebrate a free Russia on May 1, 1917. Yet with the end of the monarchy, the Russian people were undecided on a new government.

As a symbol of change in Russia, czarist emblems of the old regime are removed from buildings throughout the nation.

the royal ballet and once a close companion of the czar's. Bolshevik leaders made her house their headquarters, with a red flag flying from the roof. It was spacious and stood near an assembly hall where the Bolsheviks held political rallies. When they held their April meeting there, Lenin appeared at the conference to cheering cries of "All Power to the Soviets!"

Kschessinskaya worked to regain her house, even taking the matter to court. A judge ordered the Bolsheviks to vacate, but they remained there throughout the summer. In July, Mensheviks raided the house as they fought against the Bolsheviks. The house later became state property.

All over the city, people debated politics. Lenin's wife, Nadezhda Konstantinovna Krupskaya, later wrote,

At night I amused myself by opening the window and listening to the heated debates in a courtyard across the road from our house. A soldier was sitting there surrounded by cooks, chambermaids and I know not what other young people. At one o'clock in the morning, snatches of their talk reached me: "Bolsheviks, Mensheviks."[57]

People celebrated the first May Day as a free Russia on May 1, demonstrating in Petrograd carrying signs that read "Down with the war! Land to the Peasants! All power to the Soviets!" June brought a demonstration that attracted nearly five hundred thousand people to the streets to complain about the provisional government. The rally was called by Mensheviks and Social Democrats, but most people marched with Bolshevik signs that read "All Power to the Soviets!" "The Right to Life is Higher Than the Right to Private Property!" Others read "No Separate Peace with Germany!"

The provisional government was not able to get the large number of weapons out of civilian hands. Lenin declared that the Bolsheviks should use force to take power from the provisional government under Kerensky: "All hopes for a peaceful development of the Russian Revolution have definitely vanished."[58] Lenin and other Bolshevik leaders intended to seize control of the government through violent means, if necessary.

In August, as elections were being held, the Bolsheviks distributed propaganda aimed at winning the support of more Russians. An article in the August 15, 18, and 19 issues of *Proletarii* said, "Every worker, peasant, and soldier must vote for our list because only our party is struggling staunchly and bravely against the raging counterrevolutionary dicta-torship of the bourgeoisie and large landowners." The article declared that the Bolsheviks were the only ones struggling to maintain "the freedoms won with the blood and sweat of the people."[59] Such articles aimed to arouse anger toward those who had any property or wealth. The election gave more seats to the Bolsheviks throughout the cities.

On August 13, Kerensky spoke to the Duma, trying to keep some sort of middle ground between right and left. He said to those on the left, "Let everyone who has already tried to use force of arms against the power of the people know that such attempts will be crushed with blood and iron."[60] And to those on the right: "At the same time let those who think the time is ripe to overthrow the revolutionary government with bayonets, be even more careful."[61]

The clash between these irreconcilable viewpoints would bring more bloodshed to Russia, along with other hardships, before the revolution was complete.

7 All Power to the Bolsheviks!

The postczarist government grappled with many problems, as peasants, soldiers, and workers debated whose needs should come first. The economy had to be restructured, as did the military. Food and other goods had to be rationed and distributed.

The government faced many obstacles. For instance, workers had been demanding a shorter workday. As the government made plans to pass laws mandating an eight-hour day, soldiers protested. They themselves were risking their lives day and night at the front, they said, and needed the supplies workers could provide. Soldiers vehemently opposed shorter days for workers.

As winter approached, people lacked fuel, and mothers had no milk for their children. In Petrograd and Moscow, the bread ration was cut from one pound a day per person to one-half pound, then to one-quarter pound. Food prices doubled, and the train system broke down, which meant that grain did not arrive from Ukraine. Tens of thousands of people lost jobs as factories shut down. Inflation soared, and the amount of money circulating in the country more than doubled between January and October 1917.

Once again, wealthy Russians seemed untouched, their lives a stark contrast to those of the masses. According to American journalist John Reed, who was in Petrograd at the time, the wives of government bureaucrats had tea each afternoon with sugar and half a loaf of bread. Affluent people continued to eat in fine restaurants where they were serenaded by orchestras. Nightclubs and gambling houses remained open twenty-four hours a day. "The theatres were going every night, including Sundays. Karsavina appeared in a new ballet at the Mariinsky, all dance-loving Russia coming to see her. Chaliapin was singing . . . there were weekly exhibitions of painting," Reed wrote. Even so, he said, "the city was nervous, starting at every sharp sound."[62]

Where was Russia headed? Nobody was sure. Czarism was dead, but nothing clearly replaced it. People talked endlessly in towns and cities about politics, and rumors spread. A Siberian peasant summed up the confusion many felt: "We feel that we have escaped from a dark cave into the bright daylight. And here we stand not knowing where to go or what to do."[63]

Bolshevik Takeover

During late October, delegates to the All-Russian Congress of Soviets began arriving in Petrograd. The assembly was scheduled to meet on November 2.

November 7 dawned gray and cloudy, with a hint of sunshine. The streets of Petrograd were unusually busy. People noticed large numbers of cars, trucks, armored vehicles in the streets, and soldiers, sailors, political officials, and members of the Duma and their assistants.

In support of the Bolshevik uprising, Red Guards patrol Leningrad in an armored car.

Throughout the rest of Petrograd, children were attending school as usual, and stores, factories, and government offices were open. En route to a newspaper stand that day, a writer whose pen name was Knizhnik describes the atmosphere in Petrograd:

> As I passed the Troitsky Bridge, I saw a patrol of sailors. In the Neva, a cruiser was visible at the Nikolaevsky Bridge. In the streetcar some elderly citizen, evidently a merchant, was loudly and heatedly telling his neighbor that he was sick of the state of things, that the power of the Provisional Government was not a firm power, and therefore let even the Bolsheviks take power, if only there will be order.[64]

Knizhnik continued to wander the streets, asking people what was going on. Back home, he heard the sound of machine-gun fire. The next morning, Bolshevik trucks sped around Petrograd delivering notices that were nailed to walls throughout the city. The proclamation, written by Lenin, read:

To the Citizens of Russia!

The Provisional Government has been deposed. State power has passed into the hands of the organ of the Petrograd Soviet of Workers and Soldiers' Deputies—the Revolutionary Military Committee, which heads the Petrograd proletariat and the garrison.

The cause for which the people have fought, namely, the immediate offer of a democratic peace, the abolition of landed proprietorship, workers' control over production and the establishment of Soviet power—this cause has been secured.

Long live the revolution of workers, soldiers, and peasants![65]

That day, the Bolshevik paper *Rabochi Put* featured a long article by Lenin that urged that power be taken from the bourgeois class and given to workers and peasants. Mensheviks and Social Revolutionaries presented their views in *Izvestiya*, saying, "The Bolshevik uprising, which we have warned against as a terrible trial for the country, is being organized and started. . . . The dictatorship of one party, no matter how radical, will be as hateful to the great majority of the people as the autocracy."[66]

The Bolsheviks had failed to overthrow the government that summer. This time they were determined to prevail. They had support from disgruntled citizens who believed the Bolshevik promises of a better future. To delegates who opposed the Bolsheviks, Leon Trotsky said, "You are miserable bankrupts, your role is played out; go where you ought to go: into the dustbin of history."[67]

The Bolsheviks also had military support in the form of the Red Guard. Workers and soldiers had joined, or been recruited for, this group. During September, thousands of factory workers received rifles and military training. By October, the guard comprised twenty thousand men. Late that month, units of guards were assigned to take over, on command, the telephone exchange, railroad stations, state bank, printing plants, and bridges that spanned the Neva River.

On the night of November 7, Bolsheviks marched to Palace Square to take over the Winter Palace and arrest the ministers and overcome military cadet guards. Thousands of bullets showered the palace. The cadets could not resist this onslaught. The crowd then moved through the city to seize control of other government buildings and railway stations and arrest people.

While the Winter Palace was under siege, the Bolsheviks met in the assembly hall with the few ministers from other parties who had not fled. One of their leaders, Julius Martov, said, "The civil war is beginning, comrades! The first question must be a peaceful settlement of the crisis."[68]

As conflicts continued, the Bolsheviks sought help from more citizens. Men, women, and children were asked to help the Red Guard. They dug trenches and put up barricades and barbed wire in case Cossacks or others threatened their revolt. According to John Reed,

By tens of thousands the working people poured out, men and women; by tens of thousands the humming slums belched out their dumb and miserable hordes. Red Petrograd was in danger! Cossacks!

Twenty thousand men had joined the Red Guard by October 1917. As the new people's army, they received rifles and military training.

South and southwest they poured through the shabby streets towards the Moscovsky Gate, men, women, and children, with rifles, picks, spades, barbed wire, cartridge belts over their working clothes. . . . Such an immense outpouring of a city was never seen.[69]

There was a frenzy of activity in the palace with some soldiers looting valuables and other soldiers trying to stop them. Some soldiers and sailors began opening bottles in the imperial wine cellars and drinking the contents. Things finally became quiet inside and out in the square.

Lenin addressed Bolshevik leaders on November 8, saying, "We shall now proceed to construct the Socialist order!"[70] The Bolsheviks announced their plans: sign a peace proposal, give estate lands to peasants, de-

Women's Battalion of Death Fighters

A group of women volunteers joined the Women's Battalion of Death Regiment during World War I. The women wore plain uniforms and their hair was cut quite short, not to look masculine, but to prevent lice, parasites that infest the skin around hair and may carry dangerous diseases such as typhus. The battalion formed to carry out domestic military duties while men were at the front. They swore they would also fight against Germany until death, if necessary.

When the Bolshevik revolution began, they were sent to the Winter Palace to guard members of the provisional government, who no longer trusted other soldiers. When the fighting began, they were still inside the Winter Palace. Men in the Red Guard were ready to fire and attack, but their leader restrained them, warning them that other Russians would revile them for shooting at Russian women. After the Bolsheviks gained control of the building, the women were allowed to leave.

Members of the Women's Death Battalion volunteered to perform military duties at home while Russian soldiers fought on the front lines during World War I.

After the fall of the monarchy, Lenin called for a socialist government that would in theory distribute the nation's wealth and resources evenly among the population.

mocratize the army, allow workers to control industry, provide bread to cities and factory goods to rural areas, and create a representative assembly. Czarist institutions would be replaced by proletarian groups.

The October Decree on Land declared that all the lands once owned by the imperial family, the Russian church, and monasteries and nobles' large estates would now be under the control of district land committees and the county Soviets of Peasants' Deputies.

The Bolshevik newspaper *Pravda* had been shut down by the provisional government. Now it was published again, with headlines that read "All Power to the Soviets of Workers', Soldiers' and Peasants' Deputies! Peace! Bread! Land!" Millions of people were pleased by and enthusiastic about these decrees.

Hunger and Violence

Bolsheviks also took over Moscow, with much violence. The Kremlin was bombarded and damaged by Red Gunners on November 1.

Some Bolsheviks expressed dismay. The chief of the Department of Education, Anatoli Lunarcharsky, resigned and said,

I cannot bear this monstrous destruction of beauty and tradition. . . . Comrades, you are the new masters of this country, and although you now have many other things to reflect upon, you must also defend your artistic and scientific heritage. . . . Soon even the most uncultured among us, those whom oppression has kept in ignorance for so long, will be educated and will understand what source of joy, of strength and wisdom, are the great works of art.[71]

At the home of her aunt and uncle in Moscow, where she was attending school, Margarita Zarudny had listened to many discussions about the revolution: "In that house every word printed in the papers and press was discussed, every aspect, every pro and con. In October, when the revolution erupted and the fighting started, none of us were allowed to set foot outside the house."[72]

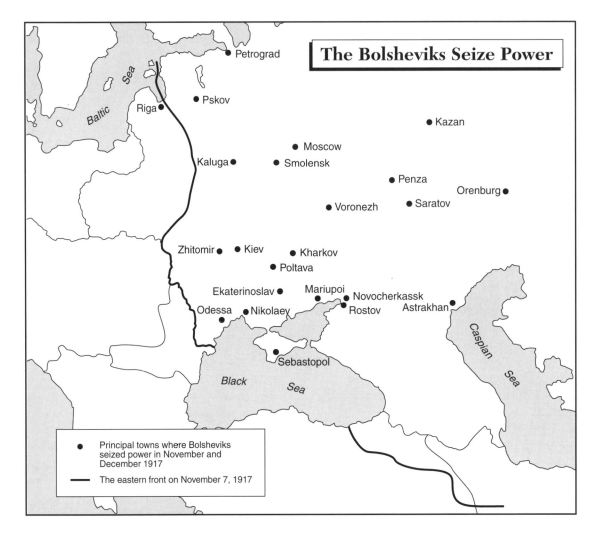

The Bolsheviks Seize Power

- Principal towns where Bolsheviks seized power in November and December 1917
— The eastern front on November 7, 1917

After the fighting between the Bolsheviks and their opponents ended, robberies and other crimes became frequent. Although her uncle was a respected professor with four children, there was little food in Zarudny's house. Some meals consisted of bits of bread with water. People exchanged belongings for food. Zarudny remembers, "One time my aunt and uncle brought home a little round sack of sunflower seeds. They'd swapped a dress for them. And so every day I'd spend a couple of hours husking sunflowers and eating seeds until I felt full."[73] In exchange for a

clock, they received a bag of oats used to feed horses. Food prices were incredibly high. Visitors from the country brought welcome gifts of food.

Violence erupted in the countryside as people attacked and killed landlords or seized land or timber plots. They took firewood and burned stores of grain and hay. Near the end of 1917, seizures of land were common. Peasants also resisted turning over grain to government officials and paying rent or taxes. In rural regions, people were impatient. Before the government completed its surveys and made recommendations, small landowners put together their own peasant soviets, or councils. Defying the laws, they stole farm tools and other items from large estates and cleared wooded areas and plowed lands that were not legally theirs.

Half of the men drafted for military service in the Russian army during the war were peasants. So since they were often peasants themselves, soldiers sent to the country to keep order seldom arrested people for these acts. The new government did not yet have an effective police force. When the peasants' actions went unchecked, they became even bolder, burning castles and manor houses.

A Family on the Run

Kyra Karadja was nine years old in 1917. She and her family were aristocrats; her father was a high-ranking government official in a medium-size town. As Bolsheviks approached their city, the family fled to the home of a local priest, knowing that they might be targets of peasant violence. Their home was ransacked by men carrying rifles and wearing red armbands. Kyra grieved to hear that the local governor had been beaten to death with rifle butts while his wife and children, whom she knew, were forced to watch.

Her mother told her and her siblings the day after they had fled, "Father is under arrest. He's given himself up. I don't yet know where he is, he's being held in one of the municipal buildings. But it's really better, he's safer this way." The family fled to the home of an aunt in Petrograd, then stayed with relatives in the Caucasus. They were eventually reunited and immigrated to the United States.

Military Deserters

Desertions continued in the army. Letters from home told soldiers that lands were being divided and given out. Many soldiers feared that they might not receive their share if they stayed with the army. By 1917, more than a million soldiers had deserted and returned to the countryside.

As the revolution spread into the military, soldiers vented their long-suppressed anger toward officers by insulting them and tearing off their medals and insignia. They refused to salute their superiors when they were off duty.

The government decreed new military procedures. Officers were ordered to stop treating soldiers rudely, although discipline was still expected. Soldiers were granted rights like other citizens.

In the months that followed, military officers said they no longer could control the troops, who disobeyed and deserted at will. Conditions in the army worsened as food deliveries ran short. Boots, more essential than ever as winter approached, were not arriving as needed. Observers said the army would collapse. A report published in 1917 called the Russian army "an exhausted mass of undernourished men in rags, full of bitterness and united only in their resentment and thirst for peace."[74] Bolshevik leaders promised them peace.

The Bolsheviks now prepared to consolidate their power and govern Russia. Sure of their convictions, they were prepared to take whatever steps were necessary to achieve their goals. It would take several more years of fighting their political enemies throughout Russia before the Bolsheviks' seizure of power was complete.

8 Blood and Iron

After the Bolshevik revolution, instability and confusion marked daily life in Russia. People in different parts of the country found themselves controlled by different forces. Bolsheviks (Reds) held Petrograd, Moscow, and most of central Russia. They were moving east. They renamed streets and cities to honor bolshevism, its leaders and ideals. Buildings were also converted for different uses, so that former mansions were now workers unions, for example.

Other areas were under anti-Bolshevik (White) control. The White army was made up of czarist officers, nobles, conservative Cossacks, peasants, bourgeois, intellectuals, and leftists who opposed bolshevism. In the south, Don Cossacks, a group of Cossacks who supported the provisional government, set up their own anti-Red government. In Ukraine, the Whites controlled the capital city of Kiev.

Shortages of food, oil, cooking equipment, nails, farm tools, textiles, matches, and many other things plagued the nation. Early in 1918, Kyra Karadja, a ten-year-old girl, lined up at a store to receive her bread ration. A man behind the counter weighed each person's piece carefully. To make her slice last longer, Karadja "took small bites and tried to count till thirty between every nibble."[75]

At noon, they might have lentils or potatoes to eat. The schools fed students tea with brown sugar and a piece of cornbread. Milk, cheese, butter, and white sugar were delicacies. Kyra and her sisters wore old dresses that they washed and pressed over and over.

Socks were carefully darned. They wore rope-soled sandals for everyday use; their shoes, worn on special occasions, were too small.

Tight Control

After the revolution, many people had hoped for a government made up of elected representatives of workers, peasants, merchants, and minorities. Early in November, people throughout Russia elected representatives for the Constituent Assembly. Out of 707 seats, 175 Bolsheviks were chosen. Another 40 seats went to Bolshevik allies. A total of 370 anti-Bolshevik Socialist Revolutionaries won seats, giving this party a majority. Voters thought these men would help to govern the nation.

This marked the first time that Russians were free to vote for their leaders. It would also be the last really free election held there for nearly seventy years. Lenin and his followers rejected a coalition government. When the elected representatives arrived in January 1918, Bolshevik guards stood outside the Tauride Palace. The Bolsheviks insisted that the group declare them the rightful leaders of Russia. When the majority of delegates refused to approve this measure, Bolsheviks and their supporters left.

The remaining delegates elected a chairman and began conducting business. They were still at work when a commander of the guards outside told the chairman they must stop for the day. When the delegates de-

In attempts to redress the exploitation of the working classes, the Bolshevik government forced the bourgeoisie to sell their possessions so that wealth could be more evenly distributed.

clined, the lights went off, and the delegates were forced to leave. The next day, they found the doors locked and armed Red Guards around the building. The elected assembly was no more.

A practical person, Lenin believed the Bolsheviks must not only take charge but render their political opponents powerless and gain support among the people. In April 1918, Lenin wrote, "We the Bolshevik Party have convinced Russia. We have *won* Russia from the rich for the poor, from the exploiters for the working people. Now we must *administer* Russia."[76]

That administration exerted tight control over people. Many new laws were passed as the government took charge of the country's banks and industries—mines, metalworks, cement, transportation, and communications, to name a few. The Bolsheviks set out to distribute goods and services and manage production. In time, workers would be subjected to numerous restrictions. Many would be told what types of jobs they must take and where they would work.

New laws dealing with social issues and family life were also enacted. All class distinc-tions were abolished, and women and men were to be treated equally. Children born within marriage or without had equal status. Civil (nonreligious) marriages were now legal.

The Bolsheviks turned large peasant farms into smaller farms. Wealthy peasants lost about 50 million hectares of land during this time, leaving them with about 30 million. Peasants were also forced to give up household goods, tools, livestock, mills, and other things without compensation. The government claimed that wealthy peasants had obtained these things by exploiting the poorer classes. However, many of these families had worked hard for generations to amass land and property. They were left with their homes and small plots of land, some belongings, equipment, and subsistence animals.

In response to criticism, the Bolsheviks claimed that they planned to store tools and the other items they seized in communal centers where people could rent and use them. However, hardly any property reached these places. It ended up in private hands.

The government also banned private renting of land and the hiring of farm laborers. Housing was nationalized.

Р.С.Ф.С.Р

ТЫ

ЗАПИСАЛСЯ
ДОБРОВОЛЬЦЕМ?

A recruitment poster for the Red Army. Lenin's government mobilized thousands of dissatisfied peasants and turned them into a military force that would scour the country, enforcing the new socialist ideals.

In April 1918, the government issued an unpopular decree that banned the right of inheritance. When someone died, his or her property would go to the state rather than heirs named by the deceased. Middle-class and wealthy Russians were incensed.

Trading laws, especially those involving food, were very strict, and offenders were severely punished. In the spring of 1918, a decree gave the officials in charge of food sweeping powers. It said that peasants were allowed to keep only the amount of grain necessary for planting and feeding their families until the next harvest. The edict blamed food shortages on "greedy peasants."

Lenin ordered thousands of men to become part of a worker's army to enforce food laws. He wrote that workers in Petrograd, for instance, must select twenty thousand people to form "a disciplined and ruthless *military* crusade against the rural bourgeoisie and against bribetakers."[77] By the end of May 1918, approximately three thousand workers were part of the "Food Army." Thousands more were part of the Military Food Bureau of the All-Russia Central Council of Trade Unions, which aided the Food Army. Few workers did this work voluntarily.

Food detachment units from the cities were sent to confiscate grain in the countryside. They were often met with strong, armed resistance. Farmers refused to give up their grain and animals. They tried hiding things before raids occurred. Some people burned their grain rather than give it to the Bolsheviks. Other families cut back production, growing only as much as they and their families would need and no more.

Bloody conflicts erupted in the grain-growing regions throughout 1918, and the Food Army suffered heavy casualties. Often, these men were not well armed or numerous enough to carry out their jobs. For years, the Bolsheviks had focused on workers. They had few party branches in farm areas. When the officials were not able to obtain as much grain as Lenin expected, he released propaganda blaming greedy peasants for hunger and starvation.

Battles between Red and White forces heated up, leading to hunger, death, and destruction in rural areas. People died of starvation. Among them was Ilya Jaffee's youngest sister. His uncle was a member of the Cheka, a type of Soviet secret police. He had brought the family from Belorussia to

Ukraine, where they would have a chance to survive. Jaffee later said,

> We traveled in a heated cattle car. When the train stopped at a station called Sinelnikov, my parents went out to buy food. My mother came back with a jug of milk and my father was carrying a big loaf of white bread that must have weighed ten pounds. They handed up the bread to my brother Misha and me. And while they were climbing back up into the cattle car, my brother and I started tearing the bread to pieces.[78]

The family was safe only briefly. The White army came, seeking Cheka members like Jaffee's uncle. When they arrived at the family's apartment, they beat Jaffee's father severely, leaving him crippled and unable to work. Jaffee recalls, "As the brightest of the five children, I had been singled out to study to become a rabbi. But now at age thirteen I went to work. Through the synagogue they found me a job in a bakery. The bread I brought home kept my family from dying of hunger."[79]

During this tumultuous period, people's attitudes toward the new government changed from confidence to distrust. Demonstrations broke out. More people turned to anti-Bolshevik parties. Workers joined the All-Russia Workers' Congress, which opposed bolshevism. These groups, joined by anarchists, decided to fight the Bolsheviks in armed conflict, if necessary, to remove them from power.

Bag Traders

The government forbade workers from going directly to farms to obtain food, a practice they called "speculating." Yet many workers were so desperate they broke the law and journeyed to farms to offer manufactured goods or handiwork in exchange for grain, potatoes, onions, and other produce. While trading in the country, some workers arranged to receive extra food by helping out on the farms, which was also illegal.

The government set up search squads and roadblocks to find these people, who faced severe penalties. The government-run press called them derogatory names like "bag traders" and *kulaks*, although most were poor or nearly poor peasants. Offenders were stripped of their grain or other products and imprisoned. Camps built to hold prisoners soon contained thousands of people.

However, many people got away with this "crime." They moved about in soldiers' uniforms, carrying guns, and looked out for each other. People also sought help from these bold men. Historian Roy Medvedev writes, "The figures indicate that without the bag traders as much as 40 percent of the population in the province might have died of hunger." The government's bread rations provided only about half of what people needed to survive. One historian later wrote,

> You could get nothing "legally" except the celebrated *vosmushka* [eighth of a pound] of bread of dubious quality and a ladleful of slops made from rotten potatoes. The entire country, including the Communists themselves, lived in violation of the Communist decrees; all of Russia "engaged in speculation," and it naturally followed that any number of official grounds could be found for "punishing each and every citizen."

Death of the Romanovs

As these conflicts grew, Bolshevik leaders worried that the czar's supporters might try to return him to power. Since March 1917, the royal family had been kept in various houses under guard. In August, they were sent to a country house in Siberia, where they stayed for eight months. A guard supervised them, but they lived quietly without incident. The czar spent his time sawing logs for fires, tending the grounds, planting vegetables, and shoveling snow. Indoors, he taught his children and read poetry with his wife. Guards expressed surprise that Nicholas was so courteous.

New and more hostile guards arrived after the Bolshevik takeover in November. Nicholas could no longer take long outdoor walks or enjoy any other exercise. The family had no funds except what some nuns smuggled in to them. The former czar's trousers

School Conflicts

Differing loyalties caused political conflicts in schools among schoolchildren as well as teachers. Young people who were loyal to the czar and the "old ways" sometimes argued with those who supported the new government. One of Kyra Karadja's older sisters, Tassia, said that she and her friends had been singing an old song during recess: "And for our Czar, Our Faith and Holy Russia, We give a loud great cheer."

Their opponents changed the last line to, "We give a loud great sneer." The conflicts escalated, and Tassia and her friends were ordered by the principal not to chant anymore. The principal, who seemed sympathetic to their beliefs, warned them they might be reported to the authorities and expelled from school.

The government organized Leagues of Young Communists for young people. They set up classes in which students were told that their religious teachings were false. Karadja wrote that in one such class, a girl dissented and argued that the man who was teaching these things was wrong. The man reacted violently, banging his fists on the table. Karadja writes, "The girl who stuck up for God wanted to leave the room because he was calling her horrid names. He would not let her; he shouted he would break her yet."

The government also put ardent Bolshevik teenagers in the schools to influence others. At the school in Tiflis where Tassia Karadja had been a student leader, a young man named Grigori Alibekoff appeared one day. He was an aggressive boy who said little in class but expounded on Bolshevik ideas between classes. Alibekoff spearheaded the organization of an atheist club and a group called Lenin's Corner in the school, and became chairman of both groups. Inside the room used as a meeting place, said Kyra Karadja, there were pictures of "priests dangling from gallows" and "posters ridiculing Christ and the Virgin Mary."

Bolshevik student groups denounced teachers and school officials who seemed partial to the old ideas. People were threatened with loss of their jobs because they had what the Bolsheviks called "undesirable social origins"—their families had belonged to the middle or upper classes. Students knew that if they protested Bolshevik ideas they might be reported to the authorities for the crime of "counter-revolutionary sentiments."

Czar Nicholas II poses here with his three daughters after his abdication. While the Bolsheviks had the Romanovs under arrest, the government was undecided whether to release the royal family or turn them over to vengeful crowds.

were patched and darned, and his shoes had been repaired many times over.

The provisional government had intended to let the Romanovs go to England as planned, but the Bolsheviks objected. Angry people did not want the czar to escape so easily. People in the Petrograd soviet were clamoring to have "Nicholas the Bloody" put on trial.

In 1918 the family was moved to Ekaterinburg, where they remained in Ipatiev House for seventy-eight days. On an upper, main floor, the children shared a bedroom, while the parents lived in another bedroom, simply furnished with two beds, an armoire with their clothing, a sofa, and two tables. A washroom and toilet were down the hall. The family ate from a common bowl of food without plates or utensils. Drinking water was ra-

tioned. They could not obtain the medicines they had been using for Alexis.

The family was always under guard, trapped behind windows painted white on the outside. Soldiers roamed their rooms, and they were forbidden to open windows or close doors, even the lavatory, nor could they contact outsiders. A priest came each Sunday to conduct mass, but guards remained during the service.

Historian Robert Massie writes,

> The family settled into a monotonous routine. They rose at nine o'clock and at ten had black bread and tea. Every morning and eve they said prayers and read from the Gospel together. Lunch was at one, dinner between four and five, tea at seven, supper at nine. Usually, Nicholas read aloud to the family after their arrival in Ekaterinburg, he read from the Book of Job. Those who wished were permitted to walk outside twice a day, thirty minutes in the morning, thirty minutes in the afternoon.[80]

Alexandra's diary shows that they spent hours sitting in the garden. Sometimes they played cards. The children helped to bake and cook in the kitchen. She herself spent much of her time caring for Alexis, but was plagued by headaches and often confined to a wheelchair because of a spinal condition.

As July arrived, anti-Bolshevik troops, including some from Czechoslovakia, were moving toward Ekaterinburg. The Bolsheviks feared that they might rescue the Romanovs. A Cheka official named Jacob Yurovsky was sent there.

On July 16, the family prayed together and had tea, as well as a special treat—fresh eggs and milk. They read the Bible before going to bed. At midnight, they were awakened and told to dress. Their captors directed them to a basement room about eleven by thirteen feet. They were then told to stand and sit together against a wall so that a photographer could take their picture.

Instead, Yurovsky said, "Your relations have tried to save you. They have failed, and we must now shoot you."[81] After shooting and bayoneting the group, the killers carried their bodies to an abandoned iron mine, where they were stripped of their clothing and jewels and dismembered. Although the bodies were soaked in acid and burned, anti-Bolsheviks who arrived in late July identified them from their charred remains. In later years, the government admitted that Bolsheviks in Moscow had ordered the massacre.

The Romanovs were not the only victims of terrorism during the civil war. Many Russians feared for their lives. The head of the Communist Party in each town had the power to arrest people. There were public trials, called courts of revolutionary justice, in which people were accused of various crimes against the Bolshevik state, then sentenced with no right of appeal. Usually, people were sentenced to death by firing squad or hanging. The sentences were sometimes carried out immediately.

People also feared the Cheka. The name stood for All-Russian Extraordinary Commission for the Struggle Against Sabotage and the Counter-Revolution. This special commission was authorized to arrest people who disrupted the new government, called "enemies of the Bolshevik regime," using terrorist tactics. Members of the Cheka had broader powers than the czar's former security squads. They acted on their own discretion, arresting people with little cause and carrying out sentences quickly, without trials. A number of the men in the Cheka were former criminals. There were rumors that the men became drunk, assaulted and robbed people, and killed innocent victims.

Strict censorship laws denied Russians the right to speak out freely or criticize the government. The Bolsheviks shut down newspapers and magazines they disliked.

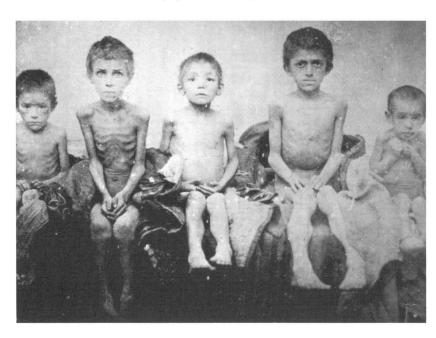

Although the government promised to feed the masses, food shortages and crop failures brought famine and disease to large sections of the population.

From the Ruins

As the civil war continued, people throughout Russia suffered more hardships and casualties as droughts and locusts ruined crops, and diseases such as typhus spread. Crime was rampant.

Industry fell apart as well. Many of the people who took charge of the factories did not know how to manage them well. There were also recurring strikes. People demonstrated against food shortages and bans on bartering for food. Workers demanded that rations be distributed equally. Bolshevik officials sent cadets from military academies into the cities to enforce a curfew. They also banned people from taking part in street demonstrations and sent armed guards to factories to impose order.

Margarita Zarudny's father was managing a steel mill in Magnitogorsk in 1918. She recalled how strikes at the blast furnaces at the mill caused chaos.

> They have to be emptied before you stop feeding them. Otherwise, a crust forms on top of the molten iron, creating a vacuum underneath. But my father and the others couldn't convince the workers of this. Blast furnaces exploded and a lot of workers were killed.[82]

The civil war resulted in many casualties. People were killed and wounded by both enemy troops and violent gangs taking advantage of the disorder. By December 1920, about 7.5 million Russians had died of starvation, illness, and exposure. Terrorism also killed many people, but these numbers remain unknown.

When the civil war ended in 1920, the country was badly damaged, with burned fields, demolished bridges, and bombed-out factories. Starvation was rampant, especially in cities. Many Russians felt disillusioned and bitter about the outcome of the revolution. The name *Bolshevik* came to be hated by many, so the party changed its name to Communist.

Poverty remained a problem for years, but progress was made in many areas of life. Roads and schools were built, and illiteracy rates declined. Health services run by the government were developed. People were encouraged to pursue the arts, and Russian scientists were highly respected.

The government continued its totalitarian methods. Every so often a purge occurred to replace unsatisfactory leaders with new ones. Officials would study the performance and records of various people and expel those who had not done what they expected.

In his 1906 book, *Results and Prospects*, Leon Trotsky wrote, "The Russian workingman will issue to all his brothers the world over his old battle cry which will now become the call for the last attack: Proletarians of the world unite!"[83]

The Bolsheviks believed Russia would lead the way as other countries adopted socialism. From socialism, they expected to proceed to communism, a total lack of private property. Said Lenin: "We have only just taken the first steps towards shaking off capitalism altogether and beginning the transition to socialism. We do not know and we cannot know how many stages of transition to socialism there will be."[84]

Convinced their view of the world was correct, these men could not know then that this economic experiment would not endure. The system would survive in various forms for about seventy years before the people of Soviet Russia demanded changes toward a more open and democratic form of government.

Notes

Introduction: A Sharp Turn in History

1. Quoted in Richard Pipes, *The Russian Revolution*. New York: Random House, 1990, p. 55.
2. Quoted in Alan Moorehead, *The Russian Revolution*. New York: Harper & Brothers, 1958, p. 8.

Chapter 1: The Czar Is Far Away: Rural Life in Czarist Russia

3. Quoted in Richard Pipes, *Russia Under the Old Regime*. New York: Random House, 1974, p. 150.
4. Quoted in Pipes, *Old Regime*, p. 351.
5. Quoted in Pipes, *Old Regime*, p. 152.
6. Quoted in Alex DeJonge, *The Life and Times of Grigorii Rasputin*. New York: Dorset Press, 1982, p. 5.
7. Quoted in DeJonge, *Rasputin*, p. xii.
8. Pipes, *Old Regime*, p. 161.
9. Pipes, *Old Regime*, p. 10.

Chapter 2: Rich Man, Poor Man: Life in Russian Cities

10. Quoted in DeJonge, *Rasputin*, p. 70.
11. Quoted in Harrison E. Salisbury, *Russia in Revolution: 1900–1930*. New York: Holt, Rinehart, and Winston, 1978, p. 18.

Chapter 3: An Iron Hand: Czarism and the Imperial Family

12. Quoted in Robert K. Massie, *Nicholas and Alexandra*. New York: Atheneum, 1968, p. 59.
13. Quoted in Pipes, *Russian Revolution*, p. 142.

14. Quoted in Massie, *Nicholas and Alexandra*, p. 16.
15. Quoted in Pipes, *Old Regime*, p. 307.
16. Editors of *Horizon* Magazine, *Russia in Revolution*. Ed. E. M. Halliday. New York: Harper and Row, 1967, p. 39.
17. Quoted in Robert K. Massie, *Peter the Great*. New York: Ballantine Books, 1980, p. 792.
18. Quoted in Massie, *Nicholas and Alexandra*, p. 19.
19. Quoted in Massie, *Nicholas and Alexandra*, p. 26.
20. Quoted in Marcel Liebman, *The Russian Revolution*. New York: Random House, 1970, p. 20.

Chapter 4: "The Czar Will Not Help Us"

21. Quoted in Liebman, *The Russian Revolution*, p. 49.
22. Quoted in Liebman, *The Russian Revolution*, p. 53.
23. Quoted in Liebman, *The Russian Revolution*, p. 52.
24. Quoted in Pipes, *Russian Revolution*, p. 355.
25. Quoted in Editors of *Horizon*, *Russia in Revolution*, p. 44.
26. Quoted in Editors of *Horizon*, *Russia in Revolution*, p. 47.
27. Quoted in Moorehead, *The Russian Revolution*, p. 53.
28. Quoted in Massie, *Nicholas and Alexandra*, p. 97.
29. Quoted in Robert Goldston, *The Russian Revolution*. Indianapolis: Bobbs-Merrill, 1966, p. 64.

30. Quoted in Moorehead, *The Russian Revolution*, pp. 57–58.

Chapter 5: Power Struggles

31. Quoted in Moorehead, *The Russian Revolution*, p. 67.
32. Quoted in Moorehead, *The Russian Revolution*, p. 74.
33. Quoted in Moorehead, *The Russian Revolution*, p. 64.
34. Quoted in Moorehead, *The Russian Revolution*, p. 74.
35. Quoted in Massie, *Nicholas and Alexandra*, pp. 180, 181.
36. Quoted in Moorehead, *The Russian Revolution*, p. 72.
37. Quoted in Massie, *Nicholas and Alexandra*, p. 176.
38. Quoted in J. S. Trewin, *The House of Special Purpose: An Intimate Portrait of the Last Days of the Russian Imperial Family*. New York: Stein and Day, 1975, p. 22.
39. Quoted in Trewin, *The House of Special Purpose*, p. 34.
40. Quoted in Moorehead, *The Russian Revolution*, p. 100.
41. Quoted in Liebman, *The Russian Revolution*, p. 80.
42. Quoted in Liebman, *The Russian Revolution*, p. 84.
43. Quoted in Liebman, *The Russian Revolution*, p. 83.
44. Quoted in Liebman, *The Russian Revolution*, p. 44.
45. Quoted in Roy Medvedev, *The October Revolution*. New York: Columbia University Press, 1979, p. 42.

Chapter 6: Peace! Land! Bread!

46. Pitirim Aleksandrovich Sorokin, *Leaves from a Russian Diary—and Thirty Years After*. Boston: Beacon Press, 1950, pp. 2–3.
47. Sorokin, *Leaves from a Russian Diary*, pp. 3–4.
48. Quoted in Liebman, *The Russian Revolution*, p. 98.
49. Quoted in Moorehead, *The Russian Revolution*, p. 135.
50. Moorehead, *The Russian Revolution*, p. 137.
51. Quoted in Moorehead, *The Russian Revolution*, p. 137.
52. Sorokin, *Leaves from a Russian Diary*, pp. 6, 7.
53. Quoted in Richard Lourie, *Russia Speaks: An Oral History from the Revolution*. New York: HarperCollins, 1991, p. 31.
54. Quoted in Moorehead, *The Russian Revolution*, p. 152.
55. Quoted in Liebman, *The Russian Revolution*, p. 107.
56. Quoted in Liebman, *The Russian Revolution*, p. 127.
57. Quoted in Liebman, *The Russian Revolution*, p. 138.
58. Quoted in Robert V. Daniels, *Red October: The Bolshevik Revolution of 1917*. New York: Scribner's, 1967, p. 41.
59. Quoted in Alexander Rabinowitch, *The Bolsheviks Come to Power: The Revolution in 1917 in Petrograd*. New York: W. W. Norton, 1976, p. 92.
60. Quoted in Rabinowitch, *The Bolsheviks Come to Power*, p. 113.
61. Quoted in Moorehead, *The Russian Revolution*, p. 161.

Chapter 7: All Power to the Bolsheviks!

62. John Reed, *Ten Days That Shook the World*. New York: Penguin, 1977, pp. 38, 76.

63. Quoted in Moorehead, *The Russian Revolution*, p. 161.
64. Quoted in Daniels, *Red October*, p. 165.
65. Quoted in Salisbury, *Russia in Revolution*, p. 155.
66. Quoted in Daniels, *Red October*, p. 166.
67. Quoted in Rabinowitch, *The Bolsheviks Come to Power*, p. 196.
68. Quoted in Daniels, *Red October*, p. 191.
69. Reed, *Ten Days That Shook the World*, p. 171.
70. Quoted in Editors of *Horizon, Russia in Revolution*, p. 120.
71. Quoted in Liebman, *The Russian Revolution*, pp. 298–99.
72. Quoted in Lourie, *Russia Speaks*, p. 40.
73. Quoted in Lourie, *Russia Speaks*, p. 41.
74. Quoted in Liebman, *The Russian Revolution*, p. 159.

Chapter 8: Blood and Iron

75. Kyra Karadja, *Kyra's Story: Reminiscences of a Girlhood in Revolutionary Russia*. New York: William Morrow, 1975, p. 77.

76. Quoted in Medvedev, *The October Revolution*, p. 127.
77. Quoted in Medvedev, *The October Revolution*, p. 154.
78. Quoted in Lourie, *Russia Speaks*, p. 49.
79. Quoted in Lourie, *Russia Speaks*, p. 50.
80. Robert K. Massie, *The Romanovs: The Final Chapter*. New York: Random House, 1995, p. 67.
81. Quoted in Massie, *Nicholas and Alexandra*, p. 491.
82. Quoted in Lourie, *Russia Speaks*, p. 61.
83. Quoted in Daniels, *Red October*, p. 24.
84. Quoted in Medvedev, *The October Revolution*, p. 131.

For Further Reading

Kathlyn and Martin Gay, *World War I*. New York: Twenty-First Century Books, 1995. Clear, absorbing account of this hugely destructive war in which Russian troops fought with Western Allies.

Robert Goldston, *The Russian Revolution*. Indianapolis: Bobbs-Merrill, 1966. Readable account of the revolution, focusing on events between 1905 and 1920; background information includes discussion of Marxism and various key political leaders.

Ronald Hingley, *A People in Turmoil: Revolutions in Russia*. New York: Julian Messner, 1970. Focuses on the social, economic, and political aspects of the revolution in 1917 and its aftermath.

Michael G. Kort, *Marxism in Power: The Rise and Fall of a Doctrine*. Brookfield, CT: Millbrook Press, 1994. A discussion of the development of Marxist ideas during the nineteenth and early twentieth centuries and the rise and fall of Marxist systems in the Soviet Union and other countries.

I. E. Levine, *Lenin: The Man Who Made a Revolution*. New York: Julian Messner, 1969. Biography of the prominent Bolshevik leader who worked tirelessly for revolution and became leader of the new Russia in 1918 and died in 1924 at age fifty-three.

Alex Nazaroff, *The Land and People of Russia*. Philadelphia: Lippincott, 1960. An overview of the history of Russia and the nation in the four decades after the revolution, focusing on its geography, resources, people, industries, agriculture, government, and daily life.

Steven Otfiniski, *Boris Yeltsin and the Rebirth of Russia*. Brookfield, CT: Millbrook Press, 1994. A look at the changing Soviet Union after the Cold War ended and people pushed for a more open and democratic society.

Abraham Resnick, *Russia: A History to 1917*. Chicago: Childrens Press, 1983. Fascinating look at czarist Russia and the way people lived in this vast land before the revolution.

Theofanis George Stavrou, ed., *Russia Under the Last Tsar*. Minneapolis: University of Minnesota Press, 1969. Describes the social and economic conditions and political climate that existed during the reign of Russia's last czar, Nicholas II.

John M. Thompson, *Revolutionary Russia, 1917*. New York: Scribner's, 1981. Close look at the events surrounding the 1917 revolution that brought down a three-hundred-year-old monarchy and changed the course of history.

Irving Werstein, *Ten Days in November: The Russian Revolution*. Philadelphia: Macrae Smith, 1967. Focuses on the Bolshevik revolution of 1917, with background information about the events that led to this momentous change.

Nancy Whitelaw, *Joseph Stalin: From President to Premier*. Columbus, OH: Silver Burdett Press, 1992. Biography of the man who rose to power in the Soviet Union after Lenin's death, ruling with an iron hand and invading Eastern Europe after World War II.

Allan K. Wildman, *The End of the Russian Imperial Army: The Old Army and the Soldiers' Revolt, March–April 1917*. Princeton, NJ: Princeton University Press, 1980. Describes how the ill-equipped, disillusioned Russian army struggled at the end of World War I and abandoned the imperial government to support the revolution.

Major Works Consulted

E. M. Almedingen, *The Romanovs: Three Centuries of an Ill-Fated Dynasty.* New York: Holt, 1966. Fascinating history of the family that reigned over Russia until the revolution in 1917.

Robert V. Daniels, *Red October: The Bolshevik Revolution of 1917.* New York: Scribner's, 1967. Detailed account of the Bolshevik takeover of Russia, following the February revolution that ended czarist rule early in 1917.

Alex DeJonge, *The Life and Times of Grigorii Rasputin.* New York: Dorset Press, 1982. Fascinating biography of the notorious "holy man" who helped to bring down a three-hundred-year-old dynasty; describes the political and social conditions that made his rise possible.

Kyril FitzLyon and Tatiana Browning, *Before the Revolution: A View of Russia Under the Last Czar.* Woodstock, NY: Overlook Press, 1978. Description of life in Russia in the decades before the revolution; illustrated with more than three hundred photographs that show Russians of various classes, ethnic groups, and professions.

Kyra Karadja, *Kyra's Story: Reminiscences of a Girlhood in Revolutionary Russia.* New York: William Morrow, 1975. Absorbing story of the day-to-day life of a young girl and her affluent family as they try to survive during the Russian Revolution.

Richard Lourie, *Russia Speaks: An Oral History from the Revolution.* New York: HarperCollins, 1991. Firsthand accounts of people from different walks of life before and during the revolutionary events of 1917; also discusses their lives after the revolution.

Robert K. Massie, *Nicholas and Alexandra.* New York: Atheneum, 1968. Detailed story of the ill-fated czar and his family, set against the monumental events that occurred between 1894 and 1918.

———, *Peter the Great.* New York: Ballantine Books, 1980. Extensive biography of one of the most famous Russian monarchs, one who ascended the throne at the age of eleven.

———, *The Romanovs: The Final Chapter.* New York: Random House, 1995. Gripping account of the massacre of the czar and his family in 1918 and the years of research and medical detective work that later verified how the entire family died that night.

Alan Moorehead, *The Russian Revolution.* New York: Harper & Brothers, 1958. Authoritative account of the people and politics of the revolution, based on many primary sources.

Edward F. Pearlstien, ed., *Revolution in Russia! as Reported by the* New York Tribune *and the* New York Herald, *1894–1921.* New York: Viking, 1967. Contains newspaper articles about current events in Russia from the time Nicholas II became czar through the revolutionary years.

Richard Pipes, *The Russian Revolution*. New York: Random House, 1990. A thorough examination of the people, politics, social issues, and events of the era; this critically acclaimed work, based on primary sources, is the work of a noted historian.

——, *Russia Under the Old Regime*. New York: Random House, 1974. Scholarly, comprehensive history of life in various cities, towns, and rural areas of Russia before the 1900s.

Alexander Rabinowitch, *The Bolsheviks Come to Power: The Revolution in 1917 in Petrograd*. New York: W. W. Norton, 1976. Focuses on events in Petrograd as the Bolsheviks swept into power.

John Reed, *Ten Days That Shook the World*. New York: Penguin, 1977. A gripping eyewitness account of the Bolshevik seizure of power in fall 1917, written by an American journalist.

Harrison E. Salisbury, *Russia in Revolution: 1900–1930*. New York: Holt, Rinehart, and Winston, 1978. Heavily illustrated, readable description of the political, economic, and social conditions that led to revolution and the first years of the Communist regime.

Leonard Schapiro, *The Russian Revolutions of 1917: The Origins of Modern Communism*. New York: Basic Books, 1984. Description of the revolution, focusing on political events and analyses.

Pitirim Aleksandrovich Sorokin, *Leaves from a Russian Diary—and Thirty Years After*. Boston: Beacon Press, 1950. Firsthand account by a man who lived in St. Petersburg (Petrograd) during the years of the revolution into the 1940s.

J. S. Trewin, *The House of Special Purpose: An Intimate Portrait of the Last Days of the Russian Imperial Family*. New York: Stein and Day, 1975. Detailed account of the czar's family, including their months in captivity, based on personal papers of Charles Sydney Gibbes, the English tutor who taught the five children and lived with them in exile; also includes personal photographs.

Additional Works Consulted

Paul Avrich, *Kronstadt 1921*. New York: W. W. Norton, 1974.

Pavel K. Benekendorff, *Last Days at Tsarskoe Selo*. Trans. M. Baring. London: Virago, 1927.

John Carey, ed., *Eyewitness to History*. Cambridge, MA: Harvard University Press, 1987.

Victor M. Chernov, *The Great Russian Revolution*. New Haven, CT: Yale University Press, 1936.

Ronald W. Clark, *Lenin: A Biography*. New York: Harper & Row, 1987.

Edward Crankshaw, *The Shadow of the Winter Palace: Russia's Drift to Revolution, 1825–1917*. New York: Viking, 1976.

Editors of *Horizon* Magazine, *Russia in Revolution*. Ed. E. M. Halliday. New York: Harper and Row, 1967.

Michael F. Florinsky, *The End of the Russian Empire*. New Haven, CT: Yale University Press, 1931.

Graeme J. Gil, *Peasants and Government in the Russian Revolution*. New York: Barnes and Noble, 1979.

Martin Gilbert, *Russian History Atlas*. New York: Macmillan, 1972.

Marcel Liebman, *The Russian Revolution*. New York: Random House, 1970.

Roy Medvedev, *The October Revolution*. New York: Columbia University Press, 1979.

Richard Pipes, *The Formation of the Soviet Union: Communism and Nationalism*. New York: Random House, 1964.

Sergei G. Pushkarev, ed., *Dictionary of Russian Historical Terms from the Eleventh Century to 1917*. New Haven, CT: Yale University Press, 1970.

Harrison E. Salisbury, *Russia*. New York: Atheneum, 1965.

Leon Trotsky, *History of the Russian Revolution*. Trans. Max Eastman. New York: Putnam, 1932.

———, *Lenin: Notes for a Biography*. New York: Putnam, 1925.

———, *1905*. New York: Putnam, 1930.

George Vernadsky et al., eds., *A Source Book for Russian History from Early Times to 1917*. 3 vols. New Haven, CT: Yale University Press, 1972.

Robert Wistrich, *Trotsky: Fate of a Revolutionary*. New York: Stein and Day, 1981.

Bertram Wolfe, *Three Who Made a Revolution*. New York: Dell, 1948.

Index

propaganda, 29, 66
Protopopov, Aleksandr, 54, 55, 57, 62
Provisional Government, 62–63, 68, 70, 71, 79

Rachmaninoff, Sergey, 26
Rasputin, Grigory Yefimovich, 50–52, 53–54
Red Cross, 52
Red Guard, 69, 70
Red Gunners, 71
religion,14, 32–33
    see also Christians; churches; Jews; Russian Orthodox Church
revolutionaries, 48, 65–66
    early revolts by, 39–41
    in exile, 47
    form terrorist groups, 29–30
    Jews as, 31
    police reaction to, 42
    see also Bolsheviks; Mensheviks
Rimsky-Korsakov, Nikolay, 26
Romanov, Alexis, 36–38, 51
Romanov, Anastasia, 37
Romanov, Olga, 37, 53
Romanov, Tatiana, 37, 53
Romanovs, 36–38, 57
    death of, 78–80
Royal Alexandrinsky Theater, 23
Royal Mariinski Theater, 23
Russia,
    culture of, 25–26
    under czarism, 30–33
    government of, 47, 48, 62–63
    growth of, 21–22
    political unrest in, 49–50, 54–55

    see also Bloody Sunday; revolutionaries
    postczarist government in, 63–66, 67–73, 74–77
    rural, 13, 18–19;
        see also peasants; serfs
    topographical characteristics of, 10
Russian Orthodox Church, 10, 20
Russian Revolution of 1917, 28, 59–63
    aftermath of, 63–66
    events leading to, 10, 11
    see also Bolsheviks
Russo-Japanese War, 42, 47

serfs, 13, 15–16
Siberia, 16, 18, 19, 25
    exiles in, 41, 43
    Romanovs in, 78
Sisters of Mercy, 53
Social Democratic Workers' Party, 41, 42, 43, 57
Social Democrats, 57, 65–66
socialism, 64, 81
soldiers, Russian, 52, 67
    desert from army, 73
    discontent with Russian government, 12, 47, 55, 56
Southern Society, 39
St. Petersburg, 22–25, 28, 50
    Marxism in, 41
    strikes in, 43
    see also Petrograd
starvation, 76–77, 81
Stolypin, Pyotr, 48–49
Stravinsky, Igor, 26
strikes, 8, 28, 52, 56
    for higher wages, 46–47
    by miners, 49–50
    by women 58

terrorism, 29–30, 40–41, 47, 81
trade, 19, 21, 76
Trans-Siberian Railroad, 21
Trotsky, Leon, 12, 47, 69
tsar. *See* czar
Tsarskoe Selo, 36, 44–45, 57

Ukraine, 18
Ulyanov, Aleksandr Ilyich, 41, 43
Ulyanov, Vladimir Ilyich. *See* Lenin
Union of Russian Factory Workers, 42
Union of Welfare, 39
unions, 48
United States, 21
universities, 40, 56
    students of, 42
upper class, 22–25, 39–40
Ural Mountains, 10

Victoria (queen of England), 33
violence, 71–73, 76, 80
    see also Bloody Sunday; terrorism

war, 52
Whites (anti-Bolsheviks), 74, 76, 77
Winter Palace, 34, 36, 45, 52
    Bolshevik takeover of, 69, 70
Women's Death Battalion, 70
working class, 12, 26–28
    aids Bolshevik takeover, 69–70
World War I, 9, 12, 52, 64, 70

Young Russia, 29

Picture Credits

Cover photo: The Bettmann Archive
Archive Photos, 17, 27 (top), 42, 50, 71
Archive Photos/Nordisk, 36
Corbis, 51
Corbis-Bettmann, 49
David King Collection, 13, 23, 25, 27 (bottom), 28, 30, 32, 34, 35, 41, 44, 45, 52, 57, 58, 59, 65, 69, 70, 75, 80

Thomas H. Hartshorne/Archive Photos, 22
Imperial War Museum/Archive Photos, 9
Library of Congress, 39, 60, 64
North Wind Picture Archives, 11
Popperfoto/Archive Photos, 79
Stock Montage, Inc., 68
UPI/Corbis-Bettmann, 24, 33, 54

About the Author

Victoria Sherrow holds B.S. and M.S. degrees from Ohio State University. Among her writing credits are numerous stories and articles, six books of fiction, and more than forty works of nonfiction for children and young adults. Her recent books have explored such topics as public education in America, the role of the media in U.S. elections, and the U.S. health care system. Sherrow lives in Connecticut with her husband, Peter Karoczkai, and their three children.